SISTERS

OF THE WAR

ALSO BY
RANIA ABOUZEID

*No Turning Back: Life, Loss, and
Hope in Wartime Syria*

SISTERS OF THE WAR

Two Remarkable True Stories
of Survival and Hope in Syria

RANIA ABOUZEID

SCHOLASTIC
FOCUS
NEW YORK

Text copyright © 2020 by Rania Abouzeid
Cover art © 2022 Sara Alfageeh

This book was originally published in hardcover by Scholastic Focus in 2020.

All rights reserved. Published by Scholastic Focus, a division of Scholastic Inc., *Publishers since 1920*. SCHOLASTIC, SCHOLASTIC FOCUS, and associated logos are trademarks and/or registered trademarks of Scholastic Inc.

The publisher does not have any control over and does not assume any responsibility for author or third-party websites or their content.

No part of this publication may be reproduced, stored in a retrieval system, or transmitted in any form or by any means, electronic, mechanical, photocopying, recording, or otherwise, without written permission of the publisher. For information regarding permission, write to Scholastic Inc., Attention: Permissions Department, 557 Broadway, New York, NY 10012.

ISBN 978-1-338-55114-3

10 9 8 7 6 5 4 3 2 1   22 23 24 25 26

Printed in the U.S.A.   23
First printing 2022

Book design by Emily Muschinske
Map by Jim McMahon

For all the children, in Syria and elsewhere,
who are forced to grow up too soon

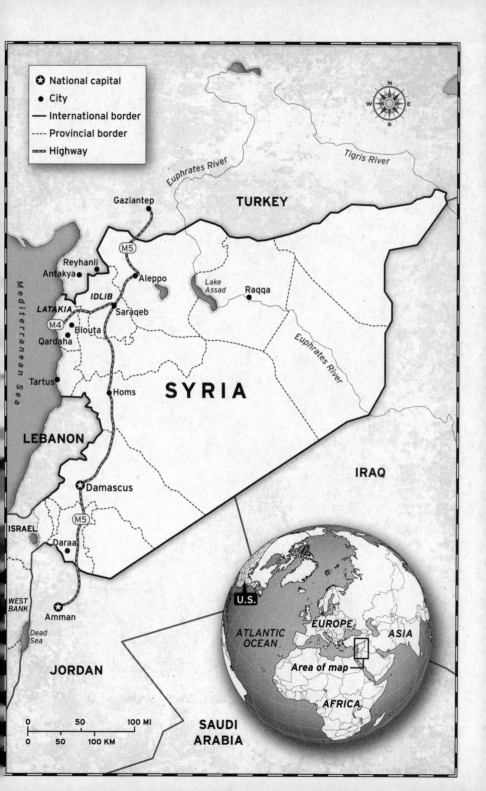

CAST OF CHARACTERS

IN SARAQEB

> **Ruha**, a nine-year-old girl [in 2011]
>
> **Maysaara** (Ruha's father) and **Manal** (Ruha's mother)
>
> **Alaa**, eight, and **Tala**, two (Ruha's sisters)
>
> **Mohammad**, five (Ruha's brother)
>
> **Zahida** (Ruha's paternal grandmother)
>
> **Mariam** (one of Ruha's seven aunts)
>
> **Mohammad** (Ruha's paternal uncle, married to Noora)

IN DAMASCUS AND BLOUTA

> **Hanin**, an eight-year-old girl [in 2011]
>
> **Talal** (Hanin's father, from Blouta in Latakia Province, living in Mezzeh 86 in Damascus) and **Awatif** (Hanin's mother)
>
> **Lojayn**, ten, and **Jawa**, six (Hanin's sisters)
>
> **Wajid** (Hanin's baby brother)

"Out of suffering have emerged the strongest souls; the most massive characters are seared with scars"

—Khalil Gibran

HANIN

The three sisters—Lojayn, Hanin, and Jawa—knew they lived in a special place, an ancient city where history wasn't confined to books; it was alive and all around them. The Syrian capital, Damascus, was one of the oldest continuously inhabited cities in the world, a place that countless generations had called home for many thousands of years. The girls—ten-year-old Lojayn, eight-year-old Hanin, and Jawa, who was almost six—didn't live in the capital's fancy parts, in its rich neighborhoods or historic districts; they lived on its fringes, on a hill in an overcrowded slum called Mezzeh 86. Still, they were proud to say they were from Damascus, even if their sliver of it was its poorer outer edge.

Relative to the grand old capital, with its long, rich

history, Mezzeh 86 was practically brand-new. It had sprouted up in the 1980s, a chaotic burst of concrete not far from the Presidential Palace. It was a messy maze of cramped buildings so close their thin outer walls kissed. The proximity and cheap building materials meant neighbors could sometimes hear conversations in other homes. It was noisy, with potholed streets that puddled in the winter, the plonk, plonk, plonk of raindrops falling on tin roofs setting off a symphony of sound. Honking drivers navigated narrow, sharply sloping two-way streets that were barely wide enough for one-way traffic. Too many people in too small a space, but to the sisters, the bustle made it feel more alive.

The family lived in a small four-room apartment off the busy main road. Their first-floor home had only one bedroom, which their parents used, so Lojayn, Hanin, and Jawa all slept in the living room on thin mattresses that doubled as floor couches during the day. The young sisters all had full rosy-red cheeks and brown eyes. They all wore their curly brown hair short but still long enough for the colorful clips and headbands and ribbons they loved to wear. They had a new baby brother, Wajid, just a few months old, who filled the small house with joy (and screams and wailing). Wajid's arrival meant Jawa was no longer the youngest child. She wasn't overly jealous or resentful of her changed status (perhaps just a bit), but she felt she'd outgrown being the baby of the family. After all, she was about to start school later that year. She looked forward to September, when she would join her sisters on the curb outside their home every morning as they waited for the minivan that would drive them to and from classes.

The older girls, Lojayn and Hanin, were also enrolled in a music school a short walk from their home, and Jawa hoped to join her sisters there, too. By early 2011, Lojayn had five years of violin lessons under her belt and was good enough to perform in two concerts with her class at the neighborhood's cultural center. Hanin's chosen instrument was the piano. She'd only just begun studying it in 2010, but it came naturally to her. "It was very easy for me," she said. Her electronic keyboard, propped on its metal stand, had pride of place in the living room. She was always careful during practice to turn the volume down in case it disturbed the neighbors, but the neighbors never complained. Jawa hadn't yet decided which instrument she wanted to play, although both of her sisters gave her lessons on their instruments. She preferred the piano to the violin.

The sisters were encouraged to express their creativity and to develop a love of the arts, both by their father, Talal, a poet, and by their mother, Awatif. Their small apartment was full of music and literature and drawings the girls made that their mother proudly taped to the walls. On occasion, Talal would read his work to his daughters. They listened in awe, not always understanding all of the words (especially Jawa) but feeling their meaning and the power of their impassioned delivery. Lojayn had even taken to writing poems of her own, hoping to emulate the father she so looked up to. Although Talal had published several books of his work, his poetry couldn't feed his family. To earn a living, he owned a small store in the neighborhood that sold perfume, cosmetics, and hair accessories.

"We used to go to Baba's store often," Hanin remembered, "and every time we drew something Baba would display it in the store to show all the customers!" The girls sometimes volunteered to stock the shelves in their spare time, for pocket money. They'd line up the hair dyes by order of number and color, smell the new perfumes, and arrange the hair accessories. Jawa usually spent her pocket money on ice cream and cookies. "They wouldn't really work; it was more like play, but they felt like they were helping out," Talal said. "We were very happy in that house. Everything was wonderful."

Outside of the girls' happy bubble, many things in Syria were less wonderful. Bashar al-Assad had been president all their lives, and Talal's daughters (at least the two older ones) knew that Bashar's late father, Hafez al-Assad, had ruled Syria as president before him. That was about the extent of what they knew about their system of governance and the Assad family's role in it.

In 1946, the same year Syria gained independence from France, a then-sixteen-year-old Hafez al-Assad joined a political organization called the Baath Party as a student activist. The next few years in Syria were a period of great instability and short-lived coups, with a parade of leaders who were overthrown and replaced. In 1952, Hafez entered the Homs Military Academy, and later graduated as an air force pilot. By 1963, he had risen through the ranks to become the head of the Syrian

Air Force. That same year, he was among a group of Baath Party supporters in the Syrian military who helped the party seize control of the country.

Syria's Baath Party, like most of the secular movements sweeping to power in the 1950s and '60s across the Middle East, preached that all citizens were equal and deserved rights and opportunities. Its idealistic guiding principles were expressed in its slogan: Unity (of the divided Arab states in the Middle East), Freedom (from foreign powers and tyranny), and Socialism (a political and economic philosophy that believes that resources and means of production should be collectively owned and distributed by a community). For Syria's Baath Party, socialism was the means by which citizens from any religious, socio-economic, or geographic background could improve their circumstances, aided by the firm guiding hand of the state. At least, that's what the party promised on paper. In reality, Syria's Baath Party, like many of the secular movements in power across the Middle East, birthed a dictatorship, and Hafez al-Assad would soon be cast in the role of dictator.

In the years after the Baath Party's 1963 takeover of Syria, growing disagreements between the party's civilian members and military members like Assad split the organization. In 1970, Hafez al-Assad snatched control of the Baath Party—and Syria—in a coup known as the Corrective Movement. He became the president of Syria, ending the period of coups and instability, and ushering in a new era—the reign of the Assads.

Hafez ruled Syria until his death in June 2000. After that, his son Bashar al-Assad became president. Before his father's death, Bashar had been living in the United Kingdom, studying to be an eye doctor, when he was summoned back to Damascus to take his father's place. He was thirty-four years old, too young by law to be president. The Syrian Constitution stated that the minimum age for a president was forty, so after Hafez's death, the Syrian parliament amended the Constitution to lower the minimum age to thirty-four, Bashar's exact age, in order for him to rule the country. That's how things worked in Syria, or "Assad's Syria" as it was often referred to, the slogan plastered on billboards and posters for decades, as if only one family could—or would—ever govern the country, as if it belonged to them. For many Syrians, not just Talal's young daughters but even adults, the Assads, both father and son, were the only leaders they had ever known. By 2011, the Assads had ruled Syria for forty-one years. And they had done so with an iron fist.

Assad's Syria was not a place with a vibrant political or civil society. Opposition of any kind was not tolerated. Syria was a one-party state, with a Constitution that Hafez al-Assad had amended in 1973 to ensure that his Baath Party "led the state and society." Nongovernmental organizations were banned (except those affiliated with the government). When the Baath Party came to power in 1963, it introduced an emergency law, a measure that was supposed to be temporary, but by 2011, it was still in place and had in reality become permanent.

Under the emergency law, protests were banned and public gatherings needed official permission. Citizens could be arrested for vaguely defined offenses such as "threatening public order" and "disturbing public confidence." Everything from private phone calls to personal letters were monitored by the state, meaning government agents eavesdropped on calls and read private mail. The media, including newspapers and television broadcasts, was censored. There was no such thing as anonymity on the internet, at least not in public places, and private internet at home was too expensive for most Syrians. Less than 1 percent of the twenty-three million Syrians in the country had broadband subscription. To get online at an internet café, a person had to hand over their national identity card and a record was kept of websites they visited. Owners could spy on their customers at any time by sharing their screens without permission. Social media sites like Facebook were blocked.

Assad's Syria was a security and military state built on its intelligence agencies—and the fear of them. There were four main agencies, known collectively as the Mukhabarat, all headquartered in the capital, Damascus, and divided into dozens of branches and sub-branches spread throughout the country, each with its own detention and interrogation facilities. They operated independently, with little low-level coordination, spying on the population—and on one another. It was assumed that the intelligence agents were always watching and listening, enforcing the emergency law, so much so that some Syrians—when they dared—privately joked that even the walls in their homes had ears. The intelligence agents, although technically supposed to be secret police acting like spies, didn't bother hiding their activities. They didn't need to. Under

Syrian law, they could not be tried in court, even "for crimes committed while carrying out their designated duties." They were, in effect, above the law. Local human rights activists and others who challenged the system disappeared in prisons, usually without their family's knowledge, sometimes for years, sometimes forever. Nobody except the state really knew how many people were behind bars, or how many more people the intelligence agents had killed. People simply went missing, their fate sometimes never known. It was difficult, if not impossible, to hold the powerful accountable, even though technically Syria held elections. The voting results were generally considered rigged and neither free nor fair. International human rights organizations called Syria a dictatorship.

Yet on the surface, despite the targeted political oppression of some citizens, Syria was an otherwise safe place. It was a country of contradictions where men and women, foreigners and locals alike, could walk home in the middle of the night without fear that a random criminal might attack them. Health care and education were free, and bread, other basic food items, fuel, and gas were subsidized, meaning the government reduced their price for the general public and paid traders the difference. At the same time, Syria was also a country corroded by corruption, where bribes were expected at every level of power, where everyday things like getting a job, or a business license, or securing a competitive place in a university program, could be made harder or easier depending on who you knew, and which officials you could bribe. Unemployment was high. Wages were low.

Despite all this, citizens knew not to complain or to try and change the system, because the cost of doing so was great. Recent history taught them so, as in 1982, when Islamists staged a mini war against Hafez al-Assad, a war they lost after Assad killed tens of thousands of people (militants and civilians alike) in the city of Hama. Or in 2004, when Syrian Kurds protested, demanding rights in a state that did not give them citizenship or let them speak or teach their Kurdish language. The state's security and intelligence arms quickly and violently crushed both incidents.

But the sisters Lojayn, Hanin, and Jawa didn't know any of that. Their parents, like many Syrians, didn't speak of such things, not even in the privacy of their own home. To the girls, their country and its capital were simply historic, beautiful places. They only knew the Damascus of tour books: the city that wore its history proudly, the place they looked forward to exploring every week. It had become something of a ritual in their home that every Friday (the first day of the weekend in Syria) the family would either go to a park or visit a historic site or a monument like the capital's famed Opera House.

The girls relished the Friday outings, especially trips to the famous markets of Souq al-Hamidieh and the adjacent Midhat Pasha Souq in the heart of the old part of Damascus. The markets themselves were relatively new—which in Damascus meant they were only a few hundred years old—but entering the pedestrian-only souqs, with their arched metal coverings, was like being transported back in time to the world of *A Thousand and One Nights*. Stores lined both sides of the souqs, the traders often standing at their front doors, inviting customers in. There was so much to experience and to see: The handwoven carpets, the delicate scarves in a rainbow of colors and fabrics, soft printed silks and robust cotton tablecloths, the elaborately embroidered and richly threaded gold and silver brocade that Damascus was famous for. Engraved copper platters that glistened when they caught the light. Pretty jewelry boxes with intricate mother-of-pearl designs and hand-carved inlaid wooden furniture. There were sacks of heaped nuts of every type and shape, often near a painter's palette of colorful spices. So many smells and sights that could make your stomach rumble. The arched black roofs covering the souqs had small irregular-shaped holes that looked like stars in the night sky. They were bullet holes from an earlier generation's fight for independence from the French, who once controlled Syria. The bullet holes had damaged the structure, but they also let in the light.

Jawa's favorite destinations were Souq al-Hamidieh and the amusement parks. "I loved all the rides, I was always so happy in the park." For Hanin, Fridays weren't complete without a stop at the famous Bakdash ice cream parlor in Souq al-Hamidieh. She loved the stretchy, almost elastic, handmade ice cream topped with pistachios that was sold year-round. The store had been in the souq since 1885 and was always crowded with customers, no matter the time of day or the season.

Damascus was a city layered with a living history. Its stones had outlasted many conquerors, from the Persians, Greeks, Romans, Byzantine, and various Islamic civilizations, as well as the French and others. Its oldest quarters were still surrounded by the remnants of Roman walls. Its monuments, like the majestic Umayyad Mosque, weren't simply roped-off relics of the past—they functioned in the present. The mosque still received worshippers, as it had for centuries. Residents still lived along narrow winding alleyways that were built well before the era of cars, or even the horse and carriage. How many people had walked the same streets that Talal and his family walked every Friday? The cobblestones had been rubbed smooth under the feet of countless generations, most of whom lived in peace but some of whom were foreigners who had come in war to conquer and control. But throughout it all, the highs and lows of its history, Damascus had remained Damascus. Back in early 2011, the three young sisters couldn't have known and wouldn't have imagined that it would be their own people—other Syrians—who would pose the greatest modern threat to their beloved ancient capital.

Talal and his wife had imparted a love of history to their daughters, but they hid some of Syria's darker history from them, like the ugliness their ancestors faced simply because of their religion. Talal's family were

Alawites, like the Assads. Alawites are a minority religious group in Syria, comprising about 11 percent of a population that is more than 70 percent Sunni Muslim. There are also Christians (who slightly outnumber Alawites), as well as small communities of Shiite Muslims, Druze, and other sects making up Syria's richly diverse society.

The Alawite religion is a very distant offshoot of Shiite Islam, although it incorporates elements of several belief systems, including Christianity, Zoroastrianism, the Druze faith, and the philosophies of Plato and Socrates. It is the type of religion that a person is born into; conversions are not permitted. Throughout their history, the Alawites were oppressed and persecuted because of their distinctive faith. Both Sunni and Shiite Muslims considered them infidels and punished them for being so. Sometimes the punishment was death. For generations, until the rise of Hafez al-Assad in the 1970s, Syria's Alawites were second-class citizens in their own country. They comprised the servant class.

Since the end of World War II, joining the military was an Alawite's main ticket out of poverty and society's fringes. Syria's elite—the wealthier Sunni merchant class and other religious communities—shunned the military as an undesirable career path, a poor man's job, so Alawites, including Hafez al-Assad, found their place in the security services. Hafez was born into a poor family in a rural village named Qardaha in the province of Latakia, part of a vast area more broadly known as the Sahel. The Sahel extended from two mountain chains near the Turkish border, down to Syria's coastal areas and the glistening waters of the Mediterranean Sea, including the country's two main port cities of Latakia and Tartus. The Sahel was Alawite heartland, the only place in the country where the demographics were reversed and sectarian minorities like the Alawites were a majority, not Sunni Muslims. Hafez al-Assad left his village in the Sahel to join the military, becoming a lieutenant who rose to command the air force by 1963. He encouraged other Alawites to enter the security forces, creating a network of uniformed men who were loyal to him, and whom, with time, he would use to grab power in the 1970 coup.

Talal and his family also traced their origins to the Sahel. They were from the village of Blouta, north of the Assads' hometown of Qardaha. Talal and his immediate family, his father and brothers, weren't military men. Like many Alawites, they were poor farmers. They lived off the land in Blouta, toiling in an apple orchard that was their only source of income. Several years of bad weather and poor harvests prompted Talal to leave his mountain home and try his luck in the big city. He moved to Damascus, where he studied and graduated from university in 2000, majoring in library and information studies. He tried and failed to find a civil service job, or any job for that matter, and so for years he sold cosmetics and hair accessories from a bag he carried on his back, going door-to-door, selling supplies to pharmacies and beauty salons and anyone else who was interested. Eventually, he saved enough money to open his small store in Mezzeh 86, and later, with the help of a bank loan, to buy the apartment that would become his family home. Blouta was still an important part of his young family's life. His wife and daughters often spent time in the village, even attending school there during extended periods, and it remained the go-to place for summer vacations.

Talal knew the stories about the religious discrimination his parents and grandparents faced, but he didn't pass them on to his daughters. Nor did he ever recall telling them that they belonged to the same religious sect as the Assads. "I wanted to plant beautiful things in my children so that they would be well-balanced and openhearted," he said, "not plant hatred and let them think, 'These other people from a different religion once oppressed my grandparents and my family, so we should respond in kind.' Never. I never wanted them to think that."

Like many Syrians, Talal and his wife believed in a secular Syria. Although Syrian society was diverse—rich in religions and ethnicities, including Kurdish, Arab, Turkoman, and Armenian—above all, it was secular, meaning that religion was secondary to the national identity that all Syrians shared. The country's official name was the Syrian Arab Republic, a designation that oppressed some non-Arab communities like the Kurds, hundreds of thousands of whom were officially stateless (even Kurds born in Syria were denied citizenship). Still, in Assad's Syria, it was considered rude to ask a person their religion, an idea reinforced by the ruling Baath Party, which believed religion had no place in the affairs of state. As far as it was concerned, faith was for the mosque or the church or any other place of worship—not the parliament and state institutions.

So it wasn't strange that Hanin and Lojayn didn't know what religion their school friends were. They also didn't know that their neighborhood in Damascus, Mezzeh 86, wasn't simply an overcrowded slum. It was considered a loyalist stronghold, a bastion of Assad supporters that was initially built near the Presidential Palace to house the families of Alawite security forces, before it allowed other Alawites like Talal to buy property there. Many men in the neighborhood were part of the security forces and members of the intelligence agencies, the men other Syrians feared, the agents who enforced the Assad regime's iron-fisted rules. But not all of them. Some were just poor Alawites like Talal who couldn't afford to live in the other, fancier parts of Damascus.

Assad's Syria may have been a secular state, but the Assads also cynically manipulated religion to prop up their power when it suited them. They surrounded themselves with trusted members of their own religious sect, elevating them to some of the most powerful positions in the state. But being Alawite wasn't an automatic ticket to greater benefits or even a guarantee of safety.

The Assads detained Alawite opponents, too. The intelligence and security forces would detain anyone who was suspected of being against the regime, regardless of religion or ethnicity or gender or age. It was one of Syria's many complicated contradictions. Damascus was safe, with little crime, but it was also a place where citizens could be detained by intelligence agents and disappear without a trace. Syria was a secular state where every citizen was supposed to be equal, regardless of religion or ethnicity, but in practice, a religious affiliation, especially if Alawite with pro-Assad politics, could provide certain advantages, and an ethnicity like Kurdish could be a disadvantage. These and many other contradictions created tensions that bubbled just below the surface of what seemed like a calm, secure Syria, contradictions that in 2011 would explode onto the streets, fueled by events elsewhere.

In early 2011, the Middle East was a very different place than it is today. It was alive with an infectious, grassroots democratic energy that had long been suppressed by dictatorial leaders. For the first time in generations, hundreds of thousands of regular citizens across the Middle East, fed up with the kings, princes, religious clerics, and civilian dictators who had lorded over them for decades, took to the streets to demand change.

It began in the North African country of Tunisia with the death of one man, Mohammed Bouazizi. He was a poor street vendor in his twenties who spent his days pushing a cart piled with produce along the dusty streets of his hometown. One day in mid-December 2010, a policewoman harassed him while he worked. It wasn't the first time he'd been bullied or intimidated by the police, but it would be the last. The officer threatened to confiscate Bouazizi's scales unless he paid a bribe that he couldn't afford. She slapped him, humiliated him, and threatened his livelihood. Enraged, Bouazizi walked to the local municipality building to complain to officials, but they refused to see him. So Bouazizi, overcome by anger, humiliation, and frustration, did something to get their attention: He set himself on fire in front of the building. The young man was hospitalized and later died from his injuries, but his desperate act ignited the anger and solidarity of hundreds of thousands of Tunisians who shared his frustrations with the corrupt ruling class and its enforcers, including the police. People filled the streets, demanding justice for Bouazizi, and an end to corruption.

The demonstrations swelled and spread across the country, quickly forcing Tunisian president Zine el Abidine ben Ali, who had been in power for twenty-three years, to flee to Saudi Arabia in mid-January 2011.

Like a wildfire, the protests spread to Egypt, Yemen, Libya, and Bahrain. A great awakening was shaking the region. The people of the Middle East, despite living in different countries, shared the same frustrations and lack of freedoms. Many unlocked voices they knew it was safer to silence, overcoming the fear of intelligence agents, prison, beatings, and even death to call for democracy, jobs, human rights, and new leaders who wouldn't punish them for speaking out. They wanted the same basic rights that people in many other countries, including the United States and those in Europe, already had and perhaps even took for granted. They dared to challenge dictators who expected to stay in power until they died, only to be replaced by their brothers or sons. These rulers who had long treated countries like their own private family businesses were now suddenly facing mass unrest and the fury of their once-cowed people.

In Egypt in mid-February, after eighteen days of protests, the country's longtime president, Hosni Mubarak, resigned. Nervous Arab leaders wondered who would be next to fall. Many sent the army and security forces out against peaceful unarmed protesters. Demonstrators were beaten, arrested, and even shot dead, but the protests continued. In the West, these momentous events were called the Arab Spring, although that's not what the people of the Middle East initially called them. The chants and protest banners and political graffiti from Tunisia to Bahrain all screamed, "Revolution!"

The revolutionary wave reached Syria in late February 2011. It began timidly, with small public gatherings, mainly candlelight vigils, in solidarity with protesters in Egypt and Libya. Although the Syrian state had no love for the leaders of Egypt, Libya, and some other Arab countries, it also didn't want Syrians demonstrating, even against those foreign leaders. Protests, after all, were banned under Syria's emergency law. More worrying for Damascus, Syrians shared many of the same frustrations being voiced in other Arab capitals—they also wanted jobs, freedoms, and dignity. If protests started in Syria, they would surely test how popular and secure President Bashar al-Assad really was.

Assad didn't seem worried (at least publicly) and wasn't

sorry to see the end of the Tunisian and Egyptian presidents. He blamed them for their own downfall, warning that this was the fate of any leader who didn't listen to his people. Assad believed he was different, and that Syria was different, because, among other things, Assad was much younger than other Arab leaders, who seemed ancient and out of touch with their majority-youth populations. In 2011, Assad was only forty-five. He was a president who seemed less stuffy and stern than other Arab leaders, who acted like pharaohs. It wasn't unusual for Assad to stroll through places like Souq al-Hamidieh with his children, stopping for ice cream like Talal's family. Assad made a point of driving his own car instead of being chauffeur driven. He casually dined in some of Damascus's best restaurants with his glamorous wife, Asma. He seemed personally approachable and likable, even if the system he headed was ruthless. At least, that was his carefully crafted image.

But things were about to change in Syria, sparked in an unlikely place, by unlikely people—a group of youths in the southern city of Daraa, near the Jordanian border. In late February, anti-regime graffiti suddenly appeared on the walls of a number of schools in Daraa. It said, *It's your turn, doctor*, referring to Assad's training as an eye doctor, and *Let the regime fall*, a modification of a protest chant that had spread across the Middle East and brought down dictators—"The people demand the fall of the regime." The security forces arrested some two dozen young men and teenagers whom they blamed for the graffiti. The Daraa children, as they came to be known in the media, weren't really children, and many had nothing to do with the writing on the walls, but their treatment in some of Syria's worst prisons and news of their torture in detention (real and embellished) sparked protests for their release in their hometown. Those protests soon spread throughout Syria, christening Daraa the birthplace of the Syrian revolution.

On March 15, 2011, the date widely considered the start of the Syrian revolution, in defiance of the emergency law, there were small demonstrations in several parts of the country, including in Daraa in the south, the city of Hasaka in the northeast, Deir Ezzor near Iraq in the east, Hama in central Syria, and even in Damascus near Souq al-Hamidieh. Amateur video captured that day in the souq showed people, no more than several dozen, clapping and walking, including a woman in a white headscarf. "Peacefully, peacefully," they chanted, as well as "God, Syria, freedom, that's all!" modifying the more common "God, Syria, Bashar, that's all!" (or Hafez, back in the day).

Talal's wife, Awatif, and daughters were in Blouta that day. Talal was often in Souq al-Hamidieh (he bought his cosmetic supplies from there), but he wasn't near the market on March 15, 2011, and so he didn't witness the protest. He later watched it on the internet, but he didn't think much of it. The gathering was small, and Syria was a security state with a powerful military. "It barely registered with me," Talal said. "It didn't mean anything." Lojayn, Hanin, and Jawa didn't see the footage and didn't know about the revolutionary movements unseating dictators elsewhere in the Middle East. They didn't follow current affairs or watch the news. They were too young, and it simply didn't interest them. The news broadcasts were full of stories about events happening elsewhere to other people; it wasn't part of their world and it didn't affect them.

It wouldn't stay that way for long.

RUHA

In another part of Syria, hundreds of kilometers to the north of Damascus, in the agricultural heartland of Idlib Province bordering Turkey, another group of sisters would soon have a very personal understanding of the revolutionary movement spreading across Syria—and the Assad regime's response to it.

Nine-year-old Ruha was the eldest of four children. She had two sisters, eight-year-old Alaa and two-year-old Tala, and a brother named Mohammad, who was five. They lived in Saraqeb, their hometown of forty thousand people, about four hours' drive from Damascus. Ruha and Alaa weren't city girls like Lojayn, Hanin, and Jawa. Their family owned and farmed great stretches of flat cinnamon-colored earth that extended like a carpet beyond the concrete clusters of their hometown. They planted fields of wheat that Ruha was sure continued forever. The little girl loved the farm, especially cucumber season. She liked plucking the small ones that her family pickled and sold.

Ruha and her family didn't live on the farm. Their home was a short drive away in the heart of Saraqeb. They weren't rich but nor were they poor; they were upper middle class, financially much better off than Lojayn, Hanin, and Jawa, who didn't even have their own bedroom. The sisters in Saraqeb, by contrast, had plenty of space. They lived in a huge family complex that was nothing like a regular house. It was more like four apartments—all spread out on the ground floor—centered around a large rectangular, open-air courtyard in the middle that connected all the living spaces. It even had a basement. It was so large that Ruha's family shared the space with her paternal grandmother, Zahida (a widow in her eighties), as well as Ruha's uncle Mohammad and his wife, Noora.

Big, traditional Syrian homes like Ruha's, built in the old style, often had an interior tiled courtyard, like a secret, private outdoor space that was invisible from the street. The courtyard was the focal point of Ruha's home; it was where she played with her siblings and where her mother, grandmother Zahida, and aunts sat and drank coffee. Unlike the girls in Mezzeh 86, who were Alawites, Ruha's family were Sunni Muslims, and all the women wore headscarves. But in the courtyard, the ladies could move around freely without covering their hair if they wanted to, enjoying the sun on their skin in total privacy, knowing that the neighbors could not see them.

Ruha's grandmother Zahida lived in a three-room section near the entrance. Ruha, her parents, and her siblings lived in an apartment to the right of the courtyard, while her uncle Mohammad and aunt Noora lived to the left. Uncle Mohammad's section even had its own smaller outdoor space, a courtyard within the courtyard. It had a beautiful marble-and-stone fountain that the family often gathered around at night, in evenings perfumed by the surrounding jasmine and rosebushes, lemon and orange trees, and grapevines that stretched overhead in a leafy canopy. The fourth, oldest part of the family complex was a lounge reserved for visitors and overnight guests. The family called it the cellar because it had thick stone walls and a high, arched ceiling that looked like an upside-down V. The cellar was so old that nobody in Ruha's family could remember which generation built it.

Ruha and Alaa shared a coral-pink bedroom stuffed with teddy bears and dolls. You could tell they were sisters just by looking at them. They had the same tight, dark brown curls that sometimes frizzed (inherited from their mother, Manal), the same large anime-like brown eyes. But Alaa was calmer by nature. Sensitive and highly imaginative, she could entertain herself for hours, whereas Ruha got bored easily. The sisters sometimes played pranks on their brother, Mohammad (who looked like a photocopy of their trim and slender father, Maysaara), but it wouldn't take long before their little brother joined in the game. Tala, the youngest child, was as cute and precious as a little china doll, with big brown eyes, porcelain-white skin, and curly, dark brown hair.

Ruha had her mother's graceful long limbs (although she was still awkwardly growing into them), her fair skin, and quiet poise, but she had inherited her father's passion, quick wit, and many of his features. They had the same bold eyebrows framing camel-like brown eyes, thick long lashes, the same full lips, and the same feistiness—although that trait surely came from Grandmother Zahida. Zahida had imparted the attitude to all of her ten children—especially her seven daughters and their daughters. Age may have stiffened Zahida's joints, reduced her hearing, and etched fine wrinkles on her still-delicate face, but it hadn't blunted her tongue or intellect. She was the formidable matriarch of a large family, a proud woman who was especially proud that all of her daughters and adult granddaughters were university educated and employed.

Ruha's aunt Mariam, in particular, was something of a trailblazer in the neighborhood. A single teacher in her fifties, she had studied in Damascus at a time when many families in Saraqeb wouldn't send their daughters to school in a nearby town, let alone to the Syrian capital four hours away. Aunt Mariam had lived in a student dorm in Damascus.

"For those with open minds, who love learning and value their daughters, it wasn't unusual," Mariam said. She returned to Saraqeb after her studies and, in early 2011, she was living with her maternal aunt, Zahida's older sister, in a three-room apartment Aunt Mariam owned above an underground gym. Mariam taught grades one to four at a local school. Ruha and her sister Alaa loved sleepovers at their aunt Mariam's because sometimes she'd let them use the gym. "We'd play on everything," Alaa said. "There were bicycles, and machines that felt like you were climbing, and a treadmill!"

Ruha's uncle Mohammad, who lived in the family complex with his wife, Noora, was Zahida's eldest son. He was a sixty-year-old environmental engineer. A slim man who wore glasses, he had a neatly trimmed mustache and salt-and-pepper-colored hair. Uncle Mohammad was the family's elder statesman, a gentle man whose voice was never raised but always respected.

Ruha's father, Maysaara, was Zahida's youngest son, the ninth of her ten children, and her clear favorite. He was thirty-nine and not as serious as his eldest brother. Maysaara was the heart of every family gathering, the one whose amusing stories everybody waited to hear. His laugh was contagious. Charismatic and reliable, Maysaara was always the first to offer help if his siblings needed it. His sisters, Ruha's aunts, often teased him that he had more shoes than his wife, Manal, and was fussier about his clothes and appearance than she was. His tailored jackets had to be just so, his shirts razor-sharp. He'd laugh at their good-natured teasing but never deny its truth. Maysaara spoiled all his children, but his eldest, Ruha, was especially dear to him. He spoke to the nine-year-old like an adult, and she carried herself with that confidence.

For Ruha, Saraqeb was her entire world because everything she loved was in it—her house, the farm, her school, her friends, and, most importantly, her family. And the heart of the extended family was Grandmother Zahida's house, at the entrance to the family complex. It was the gathering place for birthdays and holidays, especially Mother's Day, Ruha's favorite day of the year, when all seven of her aunts would visit to honor her grandmother. In early 2011, Ruha had no way of knowing and couldn't imagine that a simple knock on her front door would threaten everything and everyone she loved. But on the morning of May 1, 2011, that's exactly what happened.

She was asleep in her grandmother's bedroom. She often slept with her grandmother (she liked her cozy electric blanket) instead of in the coral-pink bedroom she shared with her sister Alaa. There was a knock on the door, loud repeated thumps that sounded angry and urgent. The noise jolted Ruha awake. She sank deeper under the bedcovers. She didn't want to answer the door. The room, the closest to the front door, was still cloaked in darkness. It was not yet dawn—too early to get up. Ruha heard water splashing in the adjacent bathroom. Her grandmother Zahida was already awake. Zahida was heavyset and moved with difficulty, slowed by illness and age, so she called out to Ruha to see who was making such a racket outside. Half-asleep, the gangly fourth grader rubbed her eyes as she approached the heavy metal door with yellow fiberglass paneling. "Who is there?" Ruha said. Nobody answered, so she cracked it open.

She saw men with guns, wearing military uniforms. They were Syrian security forces. "Where's your father?" one of the men shouted. Before she could think of an answer, Ruha's mother, Manal, raced toward her, shielding her eldest daughter behind her back as the armed men stormed into their home. "Where's your husband? He's fled, hasn't he?" Manal told them he wasn't at home.

Ruha hurried into her grandmother's living room, just steps from the front door. She was wide awake now, the fear spreading through her body like blood moving through her veins. *They're going to take Baba. I won't see my father. That's it, he won't come back,* she thought. She feared they might take her mother, too, the way she was following the men as they slammed closets, looked under beds, and searched every room. Were her siblings still asleep? If they were awake, were they as scared as she was? She felt her heart pounding like a breathless bird trapped in her chest. Grandmother Zahida prayed aloud for her youngest, favorite son: "Dear God, let Maysaara be safe. Dear God, let Maysaara be safe."

Ruha hoped her mother was telling the truth and her father wasn't home. She crept to a window. She was tall enough not to need to stand on tiptoes to see through it. It looked out onto the courtyard. Ruha watched the men in uniform raiding her home, their heavy black boots stomping across the tiled space where she played with her siblings. And then, just as suddenly as they had rushed into her house, the armed security forces stormed out—without Ruha's father. He wasn't home.

Maysaara was at a friend's house, making plans and placards for that week's demonstration. He was an anti-government protester, one of the many thousands across Syria calling for change and reform. He was on his way home when he saw truckloads of security men entering his street. He spun his car around and called his wife, Manal, then warned one of his brothers, a doctor who did not live in the family complex. It was too late for the doctor.

The dawn raid across Saraqeb on May 1, 2011, snatched thirty-eight people, including four of Ruha's uncles—three on her mother's side and her uncle the doctor, on her father's side. Grandmother Zahida let out a shriek when she learned he'd been taken. "Dear God, my son is gone! They've taken him!" she cried. Zahida couldn't hear very well but somehow always managed to hear anything about her seven daughters and three sons. Ruha usually thought her grandmother's selective hearing was funny, but there was nothing to laugh about that morning. As news of the raid spread, Ruha's aunts began gathering around her grandmother, this time not to celebrate a happy occasion like Mother's Day, but because two of Zahida's three sons were in danger. For the first time Ruha could remember, her grandmother looked scared. Zahida was in her usual spot in her living room, a faded blue couch that time had molded to her shape. She muttered to herself, as she often did, while she fished through a plastic bag of her daily medications. Uncle Mohammad was on his cell phone, calling everyone in the extended family to make sure they were safe.

Ruha looked at the telephone in her grandmother's living room. Should she call Baba? She just wanted to know if he was okay. What if he wasn't in a safe place? What if he answered and somebody heard him and he was caught because of her call? She moved between her grandmother's kitchen and the living room, where the adults had congregated, carrying water to the women. Her hands shook, but she didn't spill the liquid. At least her brother and sisters were still asleep. She was grateful that they had not witnessed what she saw.

She was worried about her father and scared about what might happen to her uncles. She'd heard the adults talk about people killed and tortured in prison. If her uncles survived, would she be able to see them in jail, the way she'd visited her maternal grandfather in 2010? She didn't know why her grandfather was imprisoned in Damascus, just that he looked older and thinner behind bars. She wondered but didn't ask. The subject made her mother cry.

Her grandfather had been arrested almost a year

earlier, on July 27, 2010, after he was overheard complaining about the cost of living and criticizing corruption. He was "invited to coffee" at 9:30 that same night by intelligence agents. Being invited to coffee or tea by the security and intelligence forces usually meant being arrested, but there was no way Ruha's grandfather could decline the "invitation." He didn't return home. The charges against him, filed in a criminal court, included weakening national morale, undermining the state, and—most hurtful to the old man—inciting sectarian strife, meaning religious hatred. He insisted the charges were all made up, that he hadn't done any of it, but it made no difference to his case. He spent almost a year in prison before he was released on bail from Damascus Central Prison in Adra on June 7, 2011. After attending a court hearing in September, he skipped the next one in November and went into hiding. He was found guilty and, although he wasn't present for the hearing, faced ten years in prison if he were ever caught.

This time, Ruha knew why her uncles were in trouble, and why the security forces wanted her father. It was because they were all serial protesters—and the government didn't want people protesting. Their home-town of Saraqeb had joined the revolutionary movement early on, and Ruha's uncles and father had partici-pated in every demonstration since Saraqeb's first, on March 25, 2011, just ten days into the revolution. It had been a small affair, no more than a few dozen men who walked, faces uncovered, from a mosque partway down the main street, chanting, "No fear after today!"

Ruha remembered how excited her father was when he returned home, how his words tumbled out. "We were all asking him, 'What did you do? What did you say?' We—my grandmother, my uncle Mohammad, and our family—were all waiting for him," Ruha said. Maysaara told her he was doing something to help Syria move forward, to secure people's rights. She knew that meant he was against the authorities. She had some idea of how "Assad's Syria" worked because of what had hap-pened to her maternal grandfather.

Maysaara was inspired to join the revolution by a sense of justice, an intolerance for corruption, and a yearning for political freedom in a system that did not allow par-ties other than the Baath. He and his family lived

comfortably, they were financially well off, but a digni-
fied life is about more than having food on the table: "I
wanted freedom," Maysaara said, "and to feel like a citizen with rights in my country."

Ruha's uncle, the doctor, spent twenty-one days in
prison. He was released, only to be arrested again two
weeks later for reasons that weren't explained to him. He
fled the country as soon as he was freed the second time.
He wasn't going to risk a third arrest. Maysaara did not
stay away from his family for long. He sneaked home
four days after the raid. His children piled on top of him,
covered him with kisses. Ruha didn't want Baba to leave,
nor did she want him to stay. She kept glancing at the
door. What if the security forces came back? Would he
have time to escape? What if they took him? She didn't
know where he had been staying and didn't want
to know. She didn't ask. The subject made her mother
cry. She wished her father would stop protesting, but she
kept that in her heart. Maysaara went into hiding after
that visit, and Ruha's life "turned upside down," as she
put it. "Baba used to stay with us all the time, then we
didn't see him anymore. We used to play on the streets,
then we started to be afraid we might be shot."

She was a little girl, but much older than a little girl. "We were fated to learn about things children shouldn't learn about," she said. "I know my parents were trying to hide things from us, but they could not. Everything was happening in front of us."

HANIN

A revolutionary protest movement was growing in a country that outlawed spontaneous protests. Across Syria, every Friday became a day of demonstrations. The marchers often set out from mosques after the Muslim Friday-afternoon prayers that are the equivalent of Sunday Mass for Christians. The mosques were the launching pads because under Syria's state of emergency law, they were among the few public places where people were allowed to gather. The spark was usually a person or group of people shouting a slogan like "The people demand the fall of the regime!" or "Death but not humiliation!" and then dozens, hundreds, and even thousands of people (in the mosque and from elsewhere) would join in, marching along a main street. Witty banners and slogans were raised, some daringly mocking

Assad and his feared intelligence agents, while others called for freedoms and human rights. Security forces— both uniformed, including the police and army, and intelligence agents in plainclothes, as well as government-affiliated thugs known as *shabiha*—often waited outside the mosques, armed with sticks, plastic whiplike rods, tear gas, and guns to terrify and prevent people from protesting. The security personnel detained men, women, and even children during demonstrations if they caught them, or they went house to house, searching for those they knew were protesting, like Ruha's father, Maysaara. They shot into crowds of unarmed demonstrators, killing many. In some parts of Syria, the enraged marchers in turn burned, felled, and destroyed some of the many statues, posters, and billboards of the Assads, both father and son, that were featured prominently in village squares, at the entrances to towns, and in government buildings, and they burned Baath Party offices and vandalized other government property.

The events were filmed and uploaded to the internet for the world to see, by young internet-savvy men and women who emerged as anti-Assad civilian activists. The activists used virtual private networks and, later, satellite phones donated by foreign supporters and smuggled into the country to bypass the government's strict controls on the internet. They even physically smuggled footage out of the country on USB drives to the neighboring states of Jordan, Lebanon, and Turkey, from where it was spread far and wide. The shaky amateur videos of protests were often broadcast on news programs around the world.

The opposition activists, who remained anonymous so that the government couldn't identify and arrest them, became points of contact for journalists who could not get into Syria to see for themselves what was happening. The activists answered media questions and shared footage. It was very difficult for journalists to get a visa to Syria, and those who did were accompanied by government minders who approved every trip or interview a journalist wanted to do, in order to try to control the story. The minders took note of what was said and done by the journalist and all those they interviewed. It made it difficult to get an accurate, unbiased picture of what was going on because some Syrians were too scared of the minders to share what they really thought and felt. (Remember, Ruha's grandfather was arrested and sentenced to ten years in prison because somebody over-heard him complaining about corruption.) Some journalists entered Syria illegally, sneaking across bor-ders to avoid the government minders and to see for themselves what the government didn't want the world to know—that there was a grassroots revolution in Syria and the Assad regime was trying to crush it.

In late March 2011, two weeks into the turmoil, President Bashar al-Assad made his first public remarks about the unrest, in a speech to the Syrian Parliament that every Syrian waited to hear. Assad had earlier sent a high-ranking delegation to Daraa, birthplace of the rev-olution, to deliver his condolences to the families of protesters killed by security forces. The local governor in Daraa (who happened to be Assad's cousin) was fired for his handling of the crisis, and the detained youths accused of writing anti-regime graffiti on school walls were released from prison.

Many Syrians, including Talal and Maysaara, hoped and expected that the president would announce reforms, like lifting the emergency law and allowing more free-doms, but instead, Assad blamed foreign conspirators and satellite television channels for encouraging the unrest. What was happening in Syria, President Assad claimed, was an attempt to sow religious hatred among the country's many diverse communities, not a call for reform. He admitted that "not all demonstrators are conspirators" and that "mistakes" had been made in Daraa, where at least sixty people had been killed in two weeks of protests, but he didn't apologize for the killings. Assad said the footage of demonstrations broadcast across the world were "lies, lies and lies that they eventually believe is the truth." He vowed that he would not "fall like a domino," like other Arab leaders being toppled by their people.

Talal was disappointed by what he heard. "It was a letdown. I had hopes that things would change, that the president's speech would change things, but it didn't. Everything—the state institutions and the way the state operated, the fear of the intelligence agencies—remained. Nothing changed." His daughters didn't watch the news or the president's speech. They continued to live in a happy bubble, unaware that a revolution was spreading across Syria.

The revolution was leaderless at the national level, although local protest leaders emerged in towns and villages, men and women who tried to organize routes for protests in their areas, who wrote the banners, like Ruha's father, Maysaara, who helped with the filming and dissemination of information, and who served as lookouts to warn others if security forces were mobilizing nearby. These local protest leaders and activists soon coalesced into groups called Local Coordination Committees, or LCCs, which often included members of prominent families in a particular area. Many towns, like Saraqeb, that were involved in the protest movement had LCCs, even if not everybody in the town supported the revolution. Sometimes the identities of the members of the LCCs were kept secret, to avoid regime retribution.

The protesters wanted an end to the emergency law and to corruption, in favor of freedom of the press and a system that allowed political parties other than the Baath Party, as well as justice and information about disappeared loved ones. They wanted economic reforms and jobs. Some wanted revenge against a system that had harmed them and their families. The Syrian state saw the protests as an existential threat to the power of Bashar al-Assad and the decades-old system of governance that his father had built. It tried to crush the peaceful movement with brute force. Security forces arrested and beat back protesters, sometimes shooting them dead. Towns like Daraa in southern Syria, home of the youth arrested (and later released) for anti-regime graffiti, the birthplace of the revolution, were punished with weeks-long sieges in which security forces did not allow any person (or anything like food) in or out of the besieged area. In the years to come, this tactic of "starve or submit" to Assad's rule would become extreme, resulting in some Syrians dying of starvation.

The regime crackdown intensified throughout 2011, pushing the death toll higher. By the summer, some soldiers and security personnel risked their lives to defect, breaking away from their units to join—and protect—protesters. It wasn't easy to defect. Security men caught trying to escape were punished, sometimes even killed, and their families were also threatened. Some of the defectors fled across Syria's northern border into neighboring Turkey, but many more tried to return to their hometowns. In some towns and villages, defectors banded together, forming armed lookouts during protests and firing back at their former colleagues if they threatened demonstrators. The same civilian activists who filmed protests also recorded defectors as they announced that they had broken away from Assad's security forces, in a bid to encourage others to do the same. The videos followed a format: A defector would announce his name, rank, and unit, stating what part of the country he had been stationed in; then he'd hold up his laminated military ID card to prove his identity.

A small group of defectors who had escaped to Turkey, led by a colonel, announced that they had formed a new rebel armed force called the Free Syrian Army. The Free Syrian Army leadership claimed that the armed men opposing Assad in Syria were all defectors, even though in reality the majority were civilians who picked up guns to defend their families, friends, and neighbors. These local armed men gathered into groups, and after a while each group started calling itself a battalion and using other military nomenclature such as brigades. The officers in Turkey said that the Free Syrian Army was organized like a regular army, with a central commander issuing orders that were followed by the armed men on the ground. In truth, it was disorganized, undisciplined, and decentralized, with defectors and armed civilians in

Syria making and following their own orders, each battalion acting on its own or in limited coordination with the few groups around it. Like the government side (and its media minders), the rebels also had a certain narrative they wanted to tell the world—as well as things they wanted to hide. Each side in Syria accused the other of lying about death tolls, about who killed whom, about the nature of the protests and their demands, in a bid to win local and international sympathy and support.

By April 2011, Assad had lifted the dreaded emergency law (but replaced it with a law just as severe) and given stateless Kurds Syrian citizenship. He ordered other reforms, but at the same time the blood of protesters continued to be spilled, fueling more demonstrations. The Syrian conflict had spiraled into a deadly cycle. Protests often resulted in people killed by the security forces. The funerals of the dead then became political gatherings (all it took was a few chants or anti-Assad speeches), gatherings that Assad's forces would violently suppress, resulting in new deaths, new funerals, new demonstrations.

Still, the revolutionary wave sweeping across Syria in 2011 didn't wash over every part of the country or all of Syria's fourteen provinces. It was strongest in rural areas like Ruha's, and much weaker, almost absent, in the big cities like the capital, Damascus, and the great northern metropolis of Aleppo, Syria's second-largest city and the economic engine of the country.

The rich merchant class of the cities stuck with the Assad regime because they benefited from that association with power. In the same way that the regime detained anyone who was against it, regardless of their sect, also in securing power, religion mattered less than politics and interests and making money (but only for those closest to the regime and for others it wanted to woo). Naturally, family came first. Bashar al-Assad's maternal cousins, the Makhloufs, became the richest and most powerful businessmen in Syria, with monopolies in telecommunications and other industries. Other people, including senior Sunni Muslim clerics and rich Sunni and Christian traders, were also given preferential treatment in Assad's Syria in exchange for their support and money.

Many other, less-influential Syrians supported Assad because they believed in the Baath Party's secular ideology, or they benefited from it, or they feared what would replace a system that had crushed alternatives. Syria's neighboring states of Iraq and Lebanon provided ugly historical examples of what wholesale state collapse looked like. It was violent and destructive. In 2003, the United States and its allies invaded Iraq to depose its dictator, Saddam Hussein, but the invasion also destroyed the country, plunging it into a vicious sectarian war between Iraq's Sunnis and Shiites and other communities. More than a million Iraqi refugees fled to Syria to escape the terror in their homeland.

Decades before the events in Iraq, from 1975 to 1990, Lebanese sectarian militias had divided and destroyed their country during a bloody civil war that pitted neighbor against neighbor. The historical memory of what had happened in Iraq and Lebanon once the leadership in those countries collapsed were not events that any Syrian (except perhaps extremists on both sides) wanted to replicate.

Damascus was largely immune to what was happening elsewhere in the country, although there were anti-Assad protests in some neighborhoods in the capital and in outlying suburbs. Damascus was heavily protected because it housed the headquarters of all the security and intelligence services and the government.

Anti-Assad opposition activists tried to get the mighty capital to rise and join their revolution. They organized *tayyar* (literally "flying"), or flash, protests that lasted fewer than ten minutes, allowing participants to escape before the security forces found them. "The aim is to get people to move," one of the activists explained. "If people protest, it will encourage others. Some residents of these areas watch us from their balconies and the women [cheer] in support. Other people curse us. It doesn't matter, it's a psychological tactic to show the regime that these areas are not as safe as it thinks. We count on the security forces then coming to those areas, setting up checkpoints, detaining people, and generally being annoying, because that will prompt the residents to demonstrate." It didn't really work.

Assad's regime launched a psychological campaign of its own. New billboards sprouted all over Damascus, sponsored by SyriaTel, a telecom firm owned by Assad's cousin Rami Makhlouf, declaring that *Syria is fine*. The message was everywhere, from talk shows on government-run television and radio stations, to billboards and food packaging. In many ways, regime-controlled parts of Syria indeed were fine. The Syrian currency, the pound, had slipped somewhat in value because of the unrest, but it was not yet a major drop. Some items were slightly more expensive in the markets, but there were no shortages and you could still buy anything you wanted if you could afford it. At the same time, large pro-Assad demonstrations were organized in the capital to counter the anti-Assad demonstrations elsewhere.

Lojayn, Hanin, and Jawa didn't know any protesters and didn't see any demonstrations. Nobody was protesting in Blouta or Mezzeh 86, either for or against the government. Their school, unlike some others, didn't bus its students into Damascus to participate in the pro-Assad rallies that were choreographed by the authorities to show support for the regime. The girls were still cocooned from the upheaval shaking Syria, and their parents didn't feel the need to expose them to reality. Why frighten them, Talal thought, especially because he believed it would soon be over anyway. "We anticipated that the state, with all its power and weight, would not fall, and would not allow these protests to continue," he said. Life carried on as normal for the family, although Talal began to hear disturbing sectarian, classist comments from some Sunni traders in Souq al-Hamidieh who sympathized with the anti-Assad opposition. "One told me, 'I swear to God we will send you back to the mountains of Latakia that you came from, and on foot!'" Talal said. "I told him, 'What do I have to do with anything, for you to say such a thing to me? I am not part of the regime.' I began to sense this from some traders and feared that things might get worse in the future, but I don't think anybody ever expected things to get as bad as they did." He had heard whispers about the kidnappings and killings of small numbers of security men, including from Mezzeh 86. The men had been snatched in undercover operations by some of Assad's opponents who had turned to violence, mirroring the brutal methods of Assad's own intelligence and security forces.

Talal kept the information, and his fears, to himself.

RUHA

Ruha didn't tell any of her friends what was happening at home, that Baba—Maysaara—didn't live there anymore, that she didn't know where he was, that he'd steal back for visits when he could. She even kept it from her best friend, Serene, with whom she walked to school every day. Serene lived at the foot of Ruha's street, at the bottom of its gentle-sloping incline.

Ruha loved Serene, a tall, fair-skinned girl with long blond hair, but she didn't trust her. Even children had picked sides in the conflict, and Serene was not on Ruha's. That wasn't the problem, because, as Ruha saw it, "everyone can have their opinion," but she thought it safer to keep hers from Serene. "I knew that if I spoke, somebody might tell their parents and might harm us, so I didn't say a word to anyone."

The blond girl was one of the many students across Syria who had participated in pro-Assad rallies. She bombarded Ruha with details of the events she'd attended. She'd recount the chants, what she wore, the route, and how much she loved the president. Ruha didn't tell her that she and her sister Alaa had twice marched with the other side. "There were a lot of children," Ruha said of her first protest, "but I didn't know if there was anyone from my class because everybody had their faces covered." Ruha, too, had covered her face with a scarf and walked with women who wore niqabs (face veils)—not because they were religiously conservative but because they wanted to conceal their identities for fear of retribution. "I knew what I was doing," Ruha said, explaining why she kept things from Serene. "We are children. If we were to speak of these things, we'd become enemies from a young age. That's wrong. I didn't want enemies."

But on one occasion, Ruha's anger got the better of her. She hit Serene and pulled her hair after Serene said that protesters were ruining the country. Serene went straight to Ruha's home and complained to Ruha's mother, Manal. "My mother apologized to her and told me off for hitting Serene. Two days later we reconciled. The problem was with the adults, not us," Ruha said. "We quickly forgot and became friends again."

As a child, Ruha had everything she wanted, but she knew older people didn't, so she marched for them. It was her decision. "When Baba participated, I decided to participate, too. Maybe if I was older, I might have been against him, on the other side, but I was young, so I walked with him." To Ruha and her sister Alaa, the demonstrations were exciting but also tinged with fear that the security forces might arrive and break things up, arrest people, or shoot into the crowd. Ruha and Alaa would clap and sing along with everyone else (there were many new pro-revolution songs) and then return home and tell the rest of the family about it.

Uncle Mohammad was terrified that something bad would happen to Ruha and Alaa at a protest, so he asked his nieces to stop going. "He was scared for us," Ruha said. "I didn't want to go to any more protests because I didn't want to break his word, and I knew he was doing it because he was looking out for our own best interests, but I also wanted to go because I thought I was participating, helping people to get what they want." The sisters obeyed their eldest uncle. Instead of attending protests, they would climb up to their flat roof and watch the demonstrators move through the streets. "They'd chant, 'God, Syria, and freedom, that's all!'" Ruha remembered.

Life at home without Baba was difficult for the girls. Maysaara's absence deeply affected all of his children, but especially his eldest daughter. Ruha's grades dropped. She didn't care for Arabic, her favorite subject. She couldn't focus in class. At night, her dreams left her afraid to close her eyes. She'd wake screaming that she had to hide Baba. The nightmares were always the same— angry knocking at the door, uniformed men swarming into her home, finding Baba, then shooting him dead in front of her. Ruha was afraid to go to school in case something bad happened at home while she was away. "After our house was raided," she said, "there were bombings in the town while we were at school." Assad's forces had escalated their response to the revolution. In addition to trying to quell the protests, they also fired artillery into unruly towns like Saraqeb, collectively punishing residents for rebelling against the regime, even if not everyone in town was against the president.

In late spring, Ruha's school was shelled during the last lesson of the day; it was English class for Ruha, math for Alaa. "It sounded like a rocket," Ruha said. "In the beginning, there were bullets," Alaa recounted, "then rockets." Soon there would be helicopter gunships and warplanes and barrel bombs and chemical weapons. It was the fate of their town, Saraqeb, to be crucified at the crossroads of two key national highways: the south–north M5 and the west–east M4. It meant that Saraqeb was smack in the middle of roads that the Syrian military used to transport supplies to its men across the country, roads that the army was determined to keep even as rebel fighters were trying to seize them.

Alaa remembered diving under her desk like all the other children the day bullets pierced the window of her classroom. She was in second grade. "Hide so you won't be shot!" her teacher yelled. Alaa found it odd that she was shivering, even though it was warm. She didn't realize it was her body's response to being afraid. Her hands couldn't blot out the ugliness of things breaking around her, even though she was pressing them as firmly as she could against her ears. Ruha and her classmates rushed to their teacher: "She hugged as many of us as she could.

We were all gathered around her in a circle, screaming, standing in the corner. I was terrified. I emptied my lungs of air."

That was the sisters' last day at school. After that, their mother and aunts homeschooled them. It was too dangerous to risk being shelled and dying in class. Ruha was happy to be home. It felt like an extended vacation, but it also meant she couldn't escape household chores. In between lessons, Aunt Mariam, the schoolteacher, taught Ruha how to knit a revolutionary-flag design onto scarves and headbands. Assad's opponents had chosen a new Syrian flag, one that had green, white, and black horizontal stripes with three red stars in the middle white stripe. (The official Syrian flag had red, white, and black horizontal stripes with two green stars in the middle white stripe.) Ruha wore the headbands around the house, especially when her father sneaked back for visits that only raised her fears that he would be captured at home.

But when the Syrian army's tanks stormed through Saraqeb on August 11 during the holy Muslim month of Ramadan, Maysaara was still in hiding. The government forces were looking for protesters. Like the first time, the second raid on Ruha's home also began in the darkness before dawn, but this time, everyone in the family was awake. They had gathered to share *suhoor*, the predawn meal ahead of the daily Ramadan fast. (In Ramadan, Muslims don't eat or drink anything, not even water, between sunrise and sunset.) Gunfire broke out, shattering the early morning quiet. "To the cellar!" shouted Ruha's mother, Manal. The children ran across the courtyard and into the arched room with thick stone walls. It was the farthest place from the front door. Manal helped her mother-in-law, Zahida, into the room. They were joined by Uncle Mohammad's wife, Noora. Uncle Mohammad wasn't there; he had gone to the farm early that day. There was no way to warn him or Maysaara because the electricity, cell phone network, and internet were cut that morning before the raid. The cellar door was left slightly open to let in light, but it also let in sound.

The hailstorm of bullets sounded as if it was getting closer. Ruha's skittish aunt Noora prayed aloud, the same words over and over: "Dear God, don't let them come in. Dear God, keep everyone safe. Dear God, protect the men." Ruha's mother flinched at every bullet, every bang, every scream. Ruha was frightened by the fear of the older women. "If we're going to die," she whispered, "at least we will die together." She knew that the regime was detaining children to lure in their wanted fathers, to force them to surrender in a cruel deal—the father's arrest for their children's release. It had happened to a three-year-old cousin on her mother's side. Let them take me, Ruha prayed, and leave my brother and sisters. Her grandmother Zahida drew her youngest grandchildren, Mohammad and Tala, into her soft belly and covered them with a blanket. "Mohammad was screaming, 'Leave me, I want to fight them!'" Ruha recalled. "We all told him to shut up."

Across town in her three-room apartment above the gym, Ruha's aunt Mariam heard wailing. Her neighbor's adult son was being dragged from his home. She sneaked to the window, parted the curtain slightly, but heard more than she could see. Her elderly neighbor was begging for his son's release.

"Get inside, old man! It's none of your business!"

Aunt Mariam crawled along the floor of her living room, afraid her silhouette would draw the men inside.

She crept up the stairs to her flat roof, peered over the edge, and saw two buses in the middle of the street, soldiers moving in and out of homes, as well as *shabiha*, the paramilitary government thugs, dressed in jeans and sneakers. She couldn't tell what was in the buses. "I saw what I thought were pillows, they were white shapes. It took me a while to realize they were men who had their undershirts pulled over their heads."

She held up her cell phone and tried to film the buses, to share evidence of what was happening, but she couldn't focus the image. Her hands were shaking. Where were her brothers? Where was Maysaara? Where were her nephews? Were they among the "pillows" in the bus? "God is with us," she murmured, whispering the words of a famous Muslim scholar to give herself strength. "And anyone who remains silent against an injustice is a mute devil." The least she could do was bear witness and pray for the men in the buses.

Back across town, Ruha froze. Banging on the front door. Her heart sank to her feet. Her mother opened the door, and uniformed soldiers swarmed in. Ruha and Alaa screamed when the men entered the cellar. They upended all the furniture and snatched from the wall a decorative 1910 musket that had belonged to Ruha's late grandfather. "Ruha started crying and asking the men to get out," Alaa remembered. "They were carrying guns."

"I breathed when they left," Ruha said. "I felt I could breathe again." It was only the first of two raids that day. The afternoon Muslim call to prayer was echoing from minarets when the second group of invaders, these not in uniform, stormed into Ruha's home. They were the *shabiha*. Some had their faces covered. "They said ugly things to Mama that made her cry," Ruha said. "They were very mean and nasty, they swore at me. They told me to shut up and stop crying. I don't know how, but I stopped. I was worried about Mama. They told Mama, 'Tell your husband to surrender to us because when we find him, we will step on his neck and break it. We will kill your brothers, too.' Mama was crying." They stole Manal's jewelry, but Maysaara had once again escaped them. Ruha's uncle Mohammad, however, was not so lucky. He was taken from the farm.

Uncle Mohammad was one of about 130 men detained in Saraqeb that day. He was imprisoned in a warehouse with hundreds of others from towns and villages across

Idlib Province. There was just one bathroom, which constantly flooded, and not enough room to lie down. The environmental engineer was embarrassed to say that he was stuck near the toilet. He slept while seated, couldn't stomach the stench to eat, and said he lost twenty kilograms in the thirty-six days he was imprisoned. The security forces insisted he had demonstrated, even though, unlike his brother Maysaara, he had not. "I was one of those who wanted dialogue with the regime," Uncle Mohammad said after he was released. "If the regime thinks that it can finish off the demonstrations by force, it is delusional, and if the opposition thinks that it can bring down the regime, it is delusional. We need to talk. I believed in that when I went to jail, and when I came out, my brother Maysaara had bought a gun."

Maysaara had done so reluctantly. "I didn't want the fall of the regime," he said. "For five months (until the August 2011 raid in Saraqeb), I didn't want its fall, just its reform, but its actions forced us to demand it. There was no armed opposition the first time the army entered Saraqeb. Nobody fought it, but after the *shabiha*, people bought guns with the idea that we wouldn't let a thug take us or anything we had."

Maysaara bought guns and ammunition for the men of his family to defend themselves, as well as for his friends and neighbors. That was how a Free Syrian Army battalion was born: a man, his brothers, cousins, nephews, friends, and neighbors armed themselves, and with time started calling themselves a battalion and using other military terms. Many battalions considered themselves part of the Free Syrian Army, while others weren't interested in being under that umbrella label.

Maysaara was also part of a secret underground network to help military defectors flee. It was as strong and as fragile as a spiderweb. The defectors were shuffled from house to house, car to car, town to town, avoiding security checkpoints by taking back roads. Maysaara became best friends with another man in this network, a businessman named Abu Rabieh, who was from a different part of Idlib Province. Abu Rabieh was gray-haired, clean-shaven, and a decade older than Maysaara. He had the LG electronics franchise in Idlib Province. They became inseparable—a pair of well-off businessmen turned revolutionaries—until one day when the violence caught up to them.

It was January 24, 2012, just before sunset. Maysaara

was driving his red Toyota HiLux pickup truck, Abu Rabieh beside him. A box of syrupy sweets slid gently along the back seat. Maysaara had pulled out of a gas station that was out of gas (outside of Damascus, there were growing shortages of many things, including gas). He drove slowly, looking for one of the many roadside fuel sellers who sold gallons of varying quality out of plastic containers. A driver in a three-car convoy stopped him to ask directions.

At the same time, Ruha was in the souq with one of her seven aunts, buying toys for her sister Alaa, who had just had an operation on her legs to correct in-toeing (or pigeon-toeing). Alaa had been terrified of the operation, but it went smoothly. When she woke in her hospital bed, she saw a teddy bear that one of her uncles had bought her. It was bigger than she was, and she wondered how she'd carry it home and where she'd put it. Ruha was debating whether or not to buy Alaa a Barbie. The dolls never lasted more than a week in her home. She didn't even bother to name them, such was their short life span. They'd break or disappear into the cupboard that Maysaara had built especially for his daughters' many teddy bears and toys. Suddenly, there was a bolt of sustained gunfire. It frightened Ruha, but her aunt told her it was on the outskirts of town. The little girl returned to examining the toys on display.

Maysaara saw the men's faces before he was pepper-sprayed. He put the truck in reverse and, temporarily blinded, drove as fast as he could toward Saraqeb as forty-eight bullets pierced the vehicle's metal skin. Drivers honked at him but swerved out of his way. He felt a burning pain in his back. "Quicker! Quicker! I'm hit, I'm hit!" Abu Rabieh kept saying. Maysaara drove until the gunfire stopped. Eyes burning, he cradled his friend's head in his lap as Abu Rabieh died in his arms.

Ruha and her aunt walked back to her grandmother's house, along with an adult male cousin they had seen at the souq. A neighbor stopped the cousin. "How is Maysaara?" he said. "God willing, he hasn't died, has he?" Ruha's feet buckled. She collapsed in the street, crying. She was inconsolable. Her cousin carried her to a house that sounded like it was in mourning. Grandmother Zahida was wailing. The old lady said she had felt like a stone was sitting on her chest all day, that something wasn't right with one of her children.

A bullet had lodged in Maysaara's back, another sliced

through him near his spine. His bloodied pants, sport jacket, and white striped shirt were returned to his family that night, but it was days before they saw him. It was raining shells when he came home, his family cowering in the cellar. Ruha's father was carried in by two men. His feet dragged behind him. The father who spoiled his children, who once drove hours just to take them to the circus, who bought their clothes from the highest-end stores, could barely speak. He could not stand. He stayed just long enough to kiss every member of his family and then was whisked away. It wasn't safe for him to linger.

Ruha was devastated. "I love my father more than I love anyone or anything," she said. "I couldn't imagine life without Baba. I wasn't thinking of anything except hoping that Baba doesn't die."

By the end of 2011, the United Nations reported that some five thousand Syrians had been killed in the revolutionary unrest. The death toll would soon spiral into the hundreds of thousands. The Syrian revolution—and the government crackdown—were very quickly becoming very ugly and violent.

RUHA

Ruha's father, Maysaara, spent months in hiding, healing from the gunshot wounds he sustained in the ambush that killed his friend Abu Rabieh. He'd been in the desert flatlands between Idlib and Raqqa under the protection of a tribal sheikh, and then spent eight weeks in Turkey. He returned home to Saraqeb on July 15, 2012. The three-car Free Syrian Army convoy of relatives that escorted him from the Turkish border honked like a wedding procession when it turned into his gently sloping alleyway.

Ruha and her siblings—Alaa, Mohammad, and Tala—waited outside their front door like coiled springs, pouncing on their father as soon as he stepped out of the car. He scooped up his two youngest, one in each arm, and walked into his mother's living room. Grandmother Zahida was in her usual spot, the faded blue couch. Maysaara knelt before her and kissed her cheeks. She took his bearded face in her hands. "Why have you come back?" she asked.

He laughed. "Is that any way to greet your son?"

"I'm happy to see you, but I'm afraid for you. You should leave."

Saraqeb had changed in his absence. It was disfigured, broken, scarred after a four-day military assault in March by Assad's men. Twenty-four civilians had been executed and more than a hundred homes burned by the security forces, including Aunt Mariam's apartment, in fires that international human rights groups said were deliberately lit. Another eleven homes were destroyed by tank fire and forty-six more were damaged but still livable. In the main souq, the corrugated-metal store shutters were peppered with bullet holes. Some were blown out and twisted into macabre art by the heat and force of explosions. No two looked alike.

On March 27, the Syrian military withdrew from Saraqeb but left behind four military posts in the town. It turned a dairy factory in the northern neighborhood and an olive oil factory in the southern neighborhood into barracks for its men. A checkpoint called Kaban was set up, and snipers were planted at an old radio communications tower. Four Free Syrian Army groups in Saraqeb opposed them, including one Maysaara helped finance, as well as other armed groups.

Not all of Assad's armed opponents identified as Free Syrian Army. Some were Islamists who wanted Syria to become an Islamic state. Many of those groups had black flags. Some battalions of the Free Syrian Army were also Islamist but not as extreme or conservative as the non-FSA groups. One non-FSA group called Jabhat al-Nusra was very secretive and strict. In Saraqeb, its small group of fighters kept to themselves and did not easily accept men who wanted to join them. With time, Jabhat al-Nusra would be exposed as Al-Qaeda's branch in Syria, but in 2012 those ties were hidden and still secret. Al-Qaeda was the group responsible for the 9/11 attacks on the United States in 2001, which destroyed New York City's iconic Twin Towers buildings, among other targets, and killed almost three thousand people.

International diplomatic efforts tried and failed to stem the bloodshed in Syria. The United Nations appointed former UN Secretary-General Kofi Annan as a special envoy to Syria. He devised a six-point peace plan that Assad said he supported. But at the same time, Syrian troops stormed Saraqeb and other towns in Idlib Province. Assad's words were one thing, the actions of his men on the ground another.

Ruha and her family fled their home during those four days of terror. Her mother and siblings, grandmother, and Uncle Mohammad and Aunt Noora escaped to their farm on the outskirts of Saraqeb, living in its cramped supply room alongside a tractor and other farm equipment, until it was safe to return to the family complex. Ruha's aunt Mariam stayed in town with one of her sisters. She couldn't sleep most nights, terrified by what she described as "ghoulish" cries and the sound of storefronts being smashed and properties looted.

Aunt Mariam lost everything in the fire. Her white plastic chairs and kitchen table melted into smooth, hard puddles. She couldn't tell whether the heaps of ash were once her clothes, cushions, quilts, or books. Her ceiling fans drooped like wilted flowers. She remembered thinking they looked beautiful. She walked out of her home with a partially melted coin collection in a metal box. That was all she kept. Her neighbors weren't allowed to put out the fire, although one tossed a hose from his kitchen window through hers. "One of my neighbors asked the security forces, 'Why are you burning the home of an old lady [Zahida's sister] and her niece?' They said, 'You don't know anything. Terrorists visit her home.' They were talking about my nephews and brothers and brothers-in-law." As far as the government was concerned, anybody who was against it, even peaceful protesters, were terrorists.

Aunt Mariam suspected that a neighbor's son had informed security forces about her family visits. She'd tutored him in the ninth grade. "I am not annoyed or upset," she said. "God compensates the oppressed. I forgive them. If it will stop here, I swear I do. Let them burn the house, we'll build something better, as long as nothing happens to any of us. We are two single women who had never protested and they burned our house. If they did that to us, what is going to happen to Syria?" Aunt Mariam and her frail aunt, Zahida's older sister, moved in with her mother, Zahida.

Ruha wore one of her best dresses—pink with yellow polka dots—the day Baba came home, but she quickly changed into the new Turkish clothes Maysaara had bought his children. She didn't even pause to take off the tags. The house was full of aunts and cousins. It felt like Mother's Day. For the first time, Ruha was relieved, not afraid, that Baba was home. "I wasn't scared because I saw that he was carrying a gun, he could defend himself a little bit," she said. "Before, he had nothing except his voice."

She knew that her father was part of something called the Free Syrian Army. She'd heard the adults talk about it. She had worried that his injuries might have permanently disabled him, but he looked the same, except for the Kalashnikov rifle that never left his side, the green ammunition vest he wore over his shirt, and the grenade he carried at all times, even during meals and when he played with his children. "I'd rather die a thousand deaths than be captured by them," he'd say. It was a common sentiment. He meant he'd rather kill himself with the grenade than be caught and imprisoned by Assad's forces. Everyone knew that prisoners were often tortured, sometimes to death, and that many of those who entered Assad's dungeons never came out, their families not knowing where they were or even if they were alive.

Maysaara may have looked the same as before, but the killing of his friend Abu Rabieh hadn't merely changed him—he said it destroyed him. "It is like a piece of shrapnel lodged in my heart," he said. "I wanted them all dead."

Saraqeb had changed and so had its people, in ways big and small, visible and invisible. The violence wounded and hardened hearts, as it did Maysaara's. It divided and destroyed communities, with people questioning whose side their friends and family were on—the revolution's or the regime's? Some of yesterday's neighbors were becoming today's enemies.

Even simple tasks like going to the souq to buy groceries were now life-and-death decisions. In Syria, markets were frequently the targets of government air strikes, and rebels also sometimes fired mortars and other artillery into civilian government-held areas. But only one side—Assad's—had warplanes and helicopter gunships and all the military might of a state. People were often killed in regime air strikes on bakeries as they waited in line for bread (there were growing shortages). Ruha's family, like every family in Syria, was forced to adjust to this new reality. So many people were dying in Syria's war that death was no longer shocking or unexpected— surviving it was. It wasn't unusual for a hundred or more people to die in a single day in violence across the country. Mourning periods, usually weeks, months, or even years long, depending on a person's relationship to the deceased, became shortened. Otherwise, as Aunt Mariam said, much of Saraqeb would be permanently draped in black. The town's Free Syrian Army fighters called ahead to the gravedigger before they went on a mission. Some paid his fee of 2,500 Syrian pounds in advance so their families wouldn't have to. Government snipers were stationed near the graveyard, hunting the bereaved, making funerals a dangerous affair. To avoid the snipers, townsfolk often buried the dead at night, hastily and with little ritual.

Every aspect of life was harder and more dangerous. There were now daily power cuts, sometimes for nine hours, sometimes for two. Nobody knew when the electricity would go out or, more important, when it would come back on. Ruha's family switched from an electric burner to a gas stove, although the gas cylinders that once cost 275 pounds were now 3,000. Bread remained at its prewar price, but the fresh produce in the market—onions, potatoes, beans, and cucumbers harvested in the fields nearby—were inflated by a factor of at least three. The family could still afford what it didn't grow. Others couldn't. Cell phone and internet coverage had been out since October 2011, but the landlines still worked. The boom of artillery fire was the new background noise. Doors were kept open so they wouldn't blow off their hinges from the force of the blasts, windows were left slightly ajar to not shatter against each other. Syrians in rebel-held areas developed a new relationship to the sky. They prayed for rain and gray stormy clouds because Assad's warplanes usually didn't fly in bad weather. After every attack on the town, Ruha's uncle Mohammad would conduct a family head count by phone to check on everyone and try to locate the strikes.

One of Maysaara's nieces and her teenage daughter, Lama, lived in Saraqeb's closest house to the old radio communications tower and its resident sniper. "He's our new neighbor," Lama joked. The sniper had shattered their windows. They repaired them with fiberglass. He shot that, too. Lama would crawl through the bedroom she shared with her single mother, certain the man with the gun could see them. He'd shot seven bullets into their bedroom door. One night, he kept firing at the thin electrical wire that attached their home to the grid until he snapped it. "I think he was bored," Lama said. After a direct rocket strike smashed a door and crushed a wall of their home, mother and daughter moved out and into the family complex with Grandmother Zahida, Uncle Mohammad and Aunt Noora, Ruha and her family, as well as Aunt Mariam and Zahida's older sister. It was getting crowded.

Aunt Mariam lived in fear of men storming their home. She took shorter showers in case she was caught naked or inappropriately dressed. Like her sisters and nieces, she began sleeping fully clothed, including in a headscarf, in case she had to quickly flee because of a bombing or a raid. But not everything changed. One afternoon, Aunt Mariam and the other women of the family sat in the inner courtyard of the family complex, joking and laughing. They picked the leaves off bundles of a green plant called *molokhia* used to make a viscous stew. The *molokhia* stalks were spread out on blankets in front of them. Ruha and Alaa helped, too. The leaves were left to dry for days before being stored for the winter *mouni*, or supplies, in a small room near the laundry. The men watched from the adjoining cellar. "Why are they bothering?" Maysaara asked. "Will we live till the winter?" One of his brothers-in-law said he no longer allowed his family to gather in the same space when the bombing intensified. He scattered his children in different rooms so that if a bomb fell, somebody, he figured, might survive.

Life in wartime meant feeling hypertense all the time, knowing that a single abrupt event—a knock on the door from the security forces, an artillery shell, or a sniper's bullet—could change everything and destroy families. It was a roller coaster of emotions, from brief moments of gleeful normality when things seemed almost as they were before the war, to terrifying fear when the planes and helicopter gunships took to the skies, to boredom because, as Alaa said, she and her siblings "weren't allowed out of the house anymore in case there was shelling or shooting," and she wanted to play outside. Now ten years old, Ruha had started to think of herself as too old to play. She passed the time, she said, by "painting my nails, listening to music, dancing, singing, and most of all, fixing each other's hair." But for now, she helped pick the leaves off the *molokhia* stalks with her female relatives. Her mother, Manal, stepped away from the courtyard and into the kitchen to do the dishes. Her eldest daughter followed her, just as a bullet hit the outer kitchen wall. Manal shuddered. "It's just a sniper," Ruha told her mother. She knew it meant one shot, not a fusillade. "Mama is so scared of bullets," Ruha said, smirking. She was embarrassed that her mother had flinched.

On Wednesday, June 18, just after lunch, one of those things happened—a single abrupt event that could change everything. It took the form of a bold, unprecedented attack on the heart of the regime in Damascus. By chance, there was electricity and the television was on, so Aunt Mariam heard the breaking news that several senior members of Assad's inner circle were killed in an explosion during a meeting at the National Security Bureau in the capital. The defense minister, the deputy defense minister (who was also Assad's brother-in-law), and the head of the president's crisis management office all died instantly. A fourth official, the director of the National Security Bureau, would later die of his wounds. It was a major blow to the government side. Aunt Mariam let out a shriek and lifted her shaking hands to her cheeks. "Thank God, thank God," she said. "Does it mean it is nearly over?"

Across Saraqeb, celebratory gunfire erupted even as some fighters in town warned their comrades not to waste the bullets. "We will need them!"

To which came the reply, "Not today!"

The gunfire intermingled with cries of *"Allahu Akbar!"* or "God is great," said in gratitude and relief, emanating from the town's mosques, along with a message to government troops in the four military outposts that was broadcast over a mosque's loudspeaker: "Your leaders are dead. You are our brothers! Join us! We will open our homes to you."

On Arabic satellite television channels, news reports poured in of defections in other parts of Syria, of soldiers and security men switching sides, of government checkpoints overrun by rebels, their booty of tanks, weapons, and ammunition falling into rebel hands. "What is wrong with us? Why haven't we done anything yet?" asked one of Mariam's nephews.

"Is it real? Is it really almost over?" another in the Free Syrian Army asked his aunt. "I'm so sick of guns, bullets, bombs."

It wasn't over. Shortly before eleven that night, a rocket plowed into the street outside the home of a family named the Breks in a different neighborhood in Saraqeb. Minutes later, a house painter appeared outside a base of rebel fighters. He was still in his beige work clothes splattered with dark green and white paint and blood. He fell to his knees, red-faced and sweaty, and opened a bloody white blanket with pale blue stripes. "People! People! Dear God! Somebody, anybody! Look what they have done! Look! Dear God, oh my God!"

The fighters ran outside. A toddler was wrapped in the blanket. She was wearing a blue T-shirt and white shorts, barefoot, with patches of blood on her pudgy legs. Her head was a squashed blob of flesh, and she no longer had a face. "She's not the only one!" the painter screamed. He collapsed, deflated, near the child, sweat and tears streaming from him. The young fighters tried to console him with words about God's will that he didn't want to hear. They told him to take the child to the town's hospital—for what, he didn't know. She was dead.

At the hospital, the little girl's mother lay dead on a stretcher, her deep red clothes soaked in blood.

Young men screamed, *"Allahu Akbar!"* this time in sorrow and anger. One swept up body bits from the floor. The rocket had killed the little girl, her mother, her brother, two aunts, and another woman from the Brek family, and wounded several others. A child in a long lilac shirt lay on the bloody floor. Her right arm was bandaged and she lay motionless, her eyes open. She looked dead but wasn't. With great effort, the little girl raised her left hand and made the "V for victory" sign.

The next day, Thursday, July 19, Saraqeb's rebels had been preparing for what they feared would be an imminent attack by government troops. Syrian state media had laid the groundwork for an offensive, reporting that Saraqeb's townspeople were asking the regime to free them of "terrorists" nested among them. Then, Wednesday's strike on Assad's inner circle reversed the momentum. Rebels across the country suddenly felt they had the upper hand and were on the verge of winning, while Assad's forces were left reeling, stunned that their enemies had penetrated the heart of Damascus and killed senior Assad officials. Saraqeb's rebels were buoyed by a sense of invincibility, or perhaps inevitability, that the shaken regime was about to fall. They decided to attack the Kaban Checkpoint, one of four outposts in their town.

The battle began at 6 p.m. The first regime tank shell landed on the home of an Assad supporter—a good omen, the rebels said. Their smugness turned to laughter when a man drove the white fire truck to put out a blaze near his home. "He's not from the fire department," a rebel said. "It's self-service."

Then, an almighty boom that sounded like a thousand cars backfiring. Rebels responded with tracer fire, the graceful arcs of red bullets reaching toward the clouds like a string of broken pearls, falling well short of the helicopter gunship circling overhead, arrogant in its altitude. Mortars crashed into concrete without any warning until seconds before impact. Shells exploded in residential streets. The helicopter gunship unleashed its rockets with a whoosh. The electricity was out, but an hour into the battle, several young civilian activists fired up a generator, hooked up an internet connection, and called nearby Free Syrian Army units via Skype, asking for help. They needed men and ammunition. "Listen, brother, the power is out here, so the line might cut. We need rocket-propelled grenades—two, three, as many as you have. Brother, it's a very difficult situation now! Mortars, tanks, and there's a helicopter, too. Whoever can come, come!"

Armed men on motorbikes roared through empty streets. Most families, including Ruha's, hid in their homes. A crowd stood outside Saraqeb's Hassan Hospital, waiting to receive the wounded. Men shouted for stretchers as cars disgorged bloodied passengers. There weren't enough stretchers, so armed locals, many in mismatched military attire and civilian clothing, carried in their wounded colleagues, or their neighbors. A man died on the street outside. His bright red blood formed a thick pool in a dip in the asphalt, as the sad, angry, frantic crowd around him cried out, *"Allahu Akbar!"*

"Tell the people that there is no more room here!" a man yelled from the hospital steps. "Send them to Shifa [Hospital]" elsewhere in town. The cars kept coming.

Broken bodies were carried in, others were carried out, mainly the dead. Grown men cried openly. The hospital floor was a mess of bloody footprints. The foyer was bursting with armed men trying to find out who was hurt, who was dead, even as the few remaining doctors shouted at them to get out to ease the overcrowding. Women asked about their sons.

A man hobbled in, unaccompanied, looking as though he'd been dipped in black soot. Two children—a little girl, her head bandaged, and her younger brother, also wrapped in white gauze—walked out of the hospital, both covered in a fine concrete dust. Their tears had mixed with the dust, creating pasty streams from their eyes to their jawlines. Within two minutes, more than a dozen people were carried in. There weren't enough gurneys, so they lay on the bloody white floor tiles.

A woman in a striped burgundy-and-navy floor-length, long-sleeved dress made her way up the few broad steps to the hospital entrance. "Where is Saddam?" she screamed to anyone, to everyone. She turned from one man to the other with the same question: "Where is Saddam? I have lost his father today, I cannot lose him, too! I want my son!" She could barely stand. She seized on a tall, middle-aged fighter with graying hair named Khaled, who wore a black ammunition vest and a Kalashnikov across his back. "Where is he?" she yelled. She grabbed him by his black vest. Khaled did not respond, could not even look at her. She slapped him across the face. "Where is my son?" Khaled turned away from the mother. Twenty minutes later, Saddam's mother ran out. "He's dead! He's dead!" she shouted. "My boy is dead!" She crumpled on the street outside the hospital, next to the pool of blood formed by the man who had died there earlier. But the following day, Saddam's mother would learn that her son was alive: A bullet had grazed his head, covering him in blood and leaving him unconscious, but he had survived.

"Empty the area, empty the area! Three tanks are moving toward us now!" The crowd outside the hospital scattered. Two teenage boys stood rooted in place, waiting with an empty orange stretcher.

Back at a Free Syrian Army outpost at a school, armed fighters trickled in from the front and the hospitals. The Kaban Checkpoint was destroyed and the fifteen or so soldiers manning it all killed. "Nobody expected this kind of retaliation," a young fighter said. "They knew where we were; why didn't they come after us instead of the families? They are cowards."

At 9 p.m., the Hassan Hospital was still receiving the wounded. A young girl no older than four or five was carried in by her father, followed by an older woman on a stretcher, and a middle-aged man. "Get out!" the doctor told an armed man who had followed them in, sobbing like a child. "She is my aunty, this is my uncle," the man said, pointing to the middle-aged couple, who were bleeding onto the floor.

The little girl begged for her mother. A nurse searched for a pair of scissors to cut away her blood-soaked pink T-shirt. "Don't be scared, my darling," the male doctor told her. The child had shrapnel in her bloodied left eye and at least two small pieces lodged in the left side of her neck, which was spurting blood. Her short black hair was in two ponytails tied with pink bands.

The base of the child's head was cut. The hospital generator hummed and sputtered and shut down three times within twenty minutes. The doctor paused, waiting for the electricity to come back on before he resumed stitching the scalp at the base of the little girl's skull. There was no anesthetic.

By 10 p.m., the death toll was twenty-five. It would climb to thirty-five. Nobody counted the wounded. The armed men outside the hospital were angry, hyped up, ready to head back and fight, but in Ruha's home, her family questioned whether the attack on the checkpoint had been worth it. "Too high a price," Aunt Mariam said, shaking her head. "So much blood. Too much blood."

The mortars and whistling rockets continued well into the night. At 12:04 a.m., one of the town's mosques broadcast a message. This time, it wasn't directed at the government troops surrounding Saraqeb, urging them to defect. It was for the townsfolk. "People of Saraqeb, there is a wounded twelve-year-old boy in the hospital. We don't know whose son he is."

The next day, Friday, July 20, another single, abrupt event occurred, the kind that could upend everything, this one also relayed in a news flash, this time just before midday. The Russian ambassador to France had declared that Assad was ready to leave office "in an orderly way."

Celebratory gunfire erupted in Saraqeb, just as it had two days earlier.

Families cooped up in their homes, including Ruha's, breathed in the streets. Neighbors congratulated each other. "Thank God, it's over," an old man in a red-and-white-checkered headdress said to himself. Women cheered and clapped. Teenage girls threw rice on fighters as they paraded through the streets. Young children dodged between vehicles to pick up spent cartridges and to gather candy tossed into the crowd. A parade snaked around town, avoiding neighborhoods with active snipers before returning to the main street near the souq. Women sprayed the crowd with water from garden hoses, providing relief from a searing midday sun.

Before an hour was up, there would be whispers that perhaps the news wasn't true, that the Syrian Information Ministry had denied the comments by the Russian ambassador. Some would murmur it, but nobody, it seemed, wanted to broadcast it openly in the crowd. The war-weary people of Saraqeb needed something to celebrate.

A man named Basil, who was a member of Maysaara's

Free Syrian Army unit, leaned on the wall of his post along the main street, puffing on a cigarette. He rested his Kalashnikov on the ground and watched the celebration. "I am crazy with happiness!" said the twenty-nine-year-old. "You know, I only picked up this gun because I was sick of hearing something called 'peaceful' while our people were being killed. I felt it was impossible to beat Bashar peacefully. Weapons were the tool, but our strength came from our community." He was a welder before he became a fighter. He said he didn't like guns, but he wasn't ready to let go of his just yet. "My gun will stay with me until we are certain that he [Assad] is gone," he said. "After that, I have two options—either I keep my weapon for my son so that he won't need to beg for a gun like his father did, or I will wait and see what becomes of this army. I will hand in my gun to the army—not Bashar's army, but the army of the Syrian Arab Republic, and I hope to never carry a gun against a Syrian again."

After forty minutes or so, the gathering thinned. Residents headed to the mosques for Friday prayers. Reality reasserted itself as people realized the news about

Assad's imminent departure wasn't true. The war wasn't over. Shelling resumed in the near distance, the familiar background noise of life in wartime.

That evening, Aunt Mariam sat outside the family's front door, watching her three nieces—Ruha, Alaa, and Tala—play in their street. It was one of the few times the girls were allowed outside. The past three days had been difficult, a roller coaster of hope and fear and feeling caged inside. The little girls crouched in their starting positions, each placing one leg in front of the other, ready to pounce on the count of three. "One, two, three!" Aunt Mariam called, and the sisters raced, giggling, to the top of their sloping narrow lane before turning around and sprinting back toward their aunt.

The night was near pitch-black, the day's heat trapped in the air. The electricity was out, as usual, so the family moved outdoors into a timid breeze. Mariam thought about the Brek family, who had suffered the rocket attack days earlier, as she watched her nieces play. "They were sitting here just like us," she said. The Brek family had been drinking tea outside their front door when a rocket fell near them. "It's frightening what we have gotten used to. Death will find us if it wants to, if God wills it, but we are changing, becoming harder as human beings." Mariam wondered when what she called "zero hour" would arrive.

"What does that mean?" Ruha asked her.

"It means when we've run out of time, when [diplomacy] and [UN Special Envoy] Annan's initiative and all the demonstrations mean nothing. When our fate will be decided," Mariam replied.

Ruha nodded. She had understood.

HANIN

The Syrian conflict was quickly drawing in foreigners on all sides—both individuals and states. Some foreigners were compelled to enter Syria and fight alongside the rebels, driven to action by the shaky amateur videos of Muslim women and children dying and begging for help. Others had different motives—they were Islamists who wanted to turn a cosmopolitan country into a conservative Islamic state. For some, religion was an afterthought, for men searching for purpose, power, adventure, or refuge from trouble back home. Some of the foreign fighters were criminals in their home countries, and Syria was a convenient escape, a cause they could claim was selfless while in reality they just wanted the power and influence that come with carrying a gun. The foreign fighters came to Syria from all over the world, from other parts of the Middle East as well as from Europe, Asia, the United Kingdom, and the United States. Some spoke Arabic and/or had Muslim or Arab backgrounds, but many others did not. Syrians in rebel-held areas, forever hospitable and increasingly desperate, accepted these foreigners, but not necessarily their ideas—especially those with conservative religious agendas.

The easiest way for foreign fighters to get into rebel-held parts of northern Syria was through Turkey. The Turkish-Syrian frontier was about 822 kilometers (or about 511 miles) long, and varied in terrain from soaring mountains to flat plains. There were smuggling routes across it that predated the war, previously used to ferry cigarettes, livestock, and other commodities between the two countries. Many were so well known they had names—the barrel, the fishery, the olives—that described something of their location or topography. They varied in length, difficulty, and terrain. There were goat tracks etched into pine-covered slopes, grassy clearings with no tree cover (you had to sprint through those sections). Routes through foliage so thick it could whip you in the face if you weren't careful. Steep climbs that tested footing on loose stones and dirt. Streams crossed by walking over fallen logs or climbing trees.

In mid-2012, after rebels snatched a number of official border posts from the Syrian regime, it became easier to travel between Turkey and Syria. Sometimes a person could openly walk through the formal crossings—even without a passport if it was a one-way trip into Syria. But other times, mainly for those headed in the opposite direction, Turkish border guards shooed Syrians back, or unleashed dogs on them, preventing them from entering Turkey. Some guards expected bribes. It was a matter of luck and the guards on duty, although in general the border was open. It was partly a humanitarian gesture to allow the thousands of Syrians escaping the war to cross into the safety of Turkey, and partly political, because the Turkish leadership at the time was against Bashar al-Assad and supported the rebels.

There were other countries, too, that in 2012 stepped up their assistance to the rebel side. The Saudis and the Qataris, along with some of their Gulf Arab allies, including the United Arab Emirates, provided weapons, ammunition, and money to their chosen rebel battalions. The United Kingdom, Europe, and the United States were also on the rebel side. There were private donors, organizations, and rich individuals like Muslim sheikhs in the Gulf or wealthy Syrians in the diaspora who financed some rebel groups. On the other side of the war, Bashar al-Assad relied on his Iranian and Russian allies who sent military advisers and in the years to come would become more actively involved in the fighting, as well as the Lebanese group Hizballah, which would soon send its disciplined fighters into battle alongside Assad's men.

Each side in the Syrian conflict was fighting for its survival in an increasingly ugly war that was not only being fought on the battlefronts but also in other arenas. There was the media war, with each side trying to tell its version of the story, as well as the language Syrians on opposite sides started using to describe each other.

Rebels referred to those on Assad's side as *shabiha*, or thugs. Assad's supporters called their opponents, whether armed rebels or peaceful protesters, terrorists. Differences in religion or financial status or political views or where a person lived were highlighted as an excuse to despise those considered "the other side." It's harder to hate and harm somebody you can relate to, so the name-calling—far from being harmless—served the dangerous purpose of demonizing Syrians on opposing sides. It classified people as either us or them, friend or foe, worthy or worthless.

The Islamists, in particular, both foreign and Syrian on the rebel side, used derogatory sectarian language to describe Alawites, claiming they were all with Assad, to deepen a religious hatred that was just another means to highlight differences between the two sides. The growing sectarianism and hate-filled language against already-frightened religious minorities like the Christians and the Alawites allowed Assad to claim that he was the protector of Syria's secular cosmopolitan society. It meant that some Syrians who feared the corruption and violence and injustice of Assad's rule nonetheless feared the alternative even more, and so they either stuck with Assad or tried to remain neutral.

Although the majority of Syrians being killed were on the rebel side, Assad's side was also sustaining losses. Posters of the regime's dead, the men forever frozen in youth, were plastered on walls, store windows, and billboards across Mezzeh 86 and other government-held

SISTERS OF THE WAR • 101

areas. Their funerals, like funerals everywhere in Syria, were communal affairs. Mezzeh 86 didn't have a grave-yard, and in any case, its inhabitants traced their origins back to their ancestral villages, mainly in and around the Sahel, so the dead were buried high in the hills of Latakia, but not before they were briefly returned to their homes in Mezzeh 86 for one last visit. Each side called its dead martyrs. The arrival of a new regime martyr was often heralded by a burst of gunfire as the flag-draped coffin was carried through the streets. Residents would emerge from their homes and stores to greet the deceased, watch-ing and wailing and sharing in a family's grief and loss, honoring their sacrifice. "The martyrs would come, weekly and sometimes daily, to our area," Talal remem-bered. His daughters didn't see or hear any funerals (they were usually at school), and he didn't feel the need to tell them about it.

More men were being drafted into Assad's war effort, although none of Lojayn or Hanin or Jawa's school friends had fathers who had newly volunteered for the military or been killed in duty. Jawa remembered hearing something on the news one day about martyrs, but she didn't understand or ask how they died. "I never watched the news, I preferred cartoons," she said. "I didn't know about anything that was happening around us."

In Syria, it was compulsory for males over eighteen years of age—with the exception of only sons—to serve twenty-one months in the military (the time period increased and decreased during the war, depending on the security situation). It was possible for a young man to delay his military service until after he finished his university studies, so some men purposely failed subjects to postpone donning a uniform. Some paid bribes to avoid conscription, but as the war dragged on, those who evaded service faced imprisonment and forced conscription if and when they were caught. In addition to the uniformed military and plainclothes intelligence agents, new volunteer paramilitary groups emerged in government-held areas. They were known as the "popular committees." By late 2012, these groups were legitimized by the state as the National Defense Forces, and given salaries. Unlike the military, in which a soldier could not choose where he was geographically stationed, members of the less-disciplined NDF patrolled their own neighborhoods. That was one of the perks of joining the NDF. Anyone could volunteer to join the militias, and in Mezzeh 86, many did. The neighborhood, like Damascus as a whole, was becoming increasingly militarized, with more armed men walking its streets.

Some of those men wore the uniform of the national army, but many of the low-level security and intelligence agents, especially the irregular forces of armed neighborhood watch–like groups, looked like many of the rebels—with their beards, and with mismatched uniforms that were partly military camouflage, partly civilian attire. The only difference was their footwear: dress shoes (often pointy-toed) for the regime men in the city, sneakers or combat boots for the rebels operating in more rugged terrain. Each side—the rebels and the regime—had its war anthems, its martyrs, its narrative, but both shared certain Syrian characteristics, like an infectious lightheartedness and bountiful hospitality—just not toward each other. But the fighting men on both sides did not think they had enough in common to spare their country further misery. They had not yet tired of killing each other, each side continuing to press ahead, certain of an outright military victory rather than a negotiated settlement. In any case, the conflict was no longer just about Syrians, given all the regional and international players on each side of the war.

Damascus, the wondrous capital beloved by Talal's daughters, increasingly felt like a tired and scared old man, sagging under the weight of new burdens. Thousands of people who had been displaced by fighting in other parts of the country had flooded into the capital. Many were housed in schools that were turned into shelters while those who could afford it lived in hotel rooms at discounted rates. They didn't have a problem finding a hotel room—the tourists were staying away. The capital had become a city of barricades, choked by concrete checkpoints that snarled traffic. Thigh-high barriers, painted in the state's two-starred flag, and concrete blast walls blocked key roads leading to government offices, turning the areas into no-go zones. Damascus was a city that had at once expanded due to the human influx but also had shrunk in terms of the number of roads and areas accessible to regular citizens. Things that were not present before were becoming common, like the men of the NDF manning small checkpoints that were often little more than a thin flagpole in the middle of narrow neighborhood streets. The men were armed with Kalashnikov rifles, black walkie-talkies, and often fake bomb detectors that looked like a thin metal antenna, which was supposed to bend like a divining rod when it detected explosives. (In reality the devices didn't work, and the two British businessmen who invented and sold the wands were sentenced to prison in the United Kingdom for fraud. Nonetheless, the devices were still in use, not just in Syria, but across the Middle East.)

Mezzeh 86, like the rest of Damascus, had also changed. There were new checkpoints at the foot of the hill leading up to the neighborhood, and checkpoints within it. Armed men and soldiers roamed the tight two-way streets. The faces of the dead (as well as images of the president) stared out from every conceivable surface. The increased armed presence and checkpoints didn't frighten Lojayn, Hanin, and Jawa. "When we used to stop at a checkpoint, we'd start singing or we'd chant, 'God, Syria, and Bashar, that's all!'" Jawa said. "We weren't scared." She and her sisters still didn't know about the revolution, or the anti-Assad protests, or that there was something called a Free Syrian Army and other, non-FSA Islamist battalions, or what was really happening in the country. Their blissful bubble had not yet burst.

For their father, Talal, the checkpoints were a physical reminder of the deteriorating security situation. "The checkpoints were everywhere. The capital had changed. The general mood had changed. There was fear, concern, anxiety."

Mezzeh 86 had suffered several mortar attacks, the rockets fired from nearby rebel-held areas on the outskirts of Damascus. One of the mortar rounds landed in the neighborhood by accident. The rebels had aimed at the nearby Presidential Palace but missed their target, hitting Mezzeh 86 and killing three people and wounding seven others. And then, there was the car bomb that sneaked into the overcrowded neighborhood in the first week of November 2012.

It happened late in the afternoon on a cool winter's day. Talal was in his store, serving customers, when a boom he said was "stronger than any sound I had ever heard in my life" shook him to his core. The force of the blast dislodged items from the shelves, although later Talal couldn't be sure if some of the sunglasses and watches scattered across the floor fell because of the blast or the female customers, who in their fright knocked them over. Talal stood frozen in place, unsure of what had just happened: "What is this? Where is it? Is it a rocket or a car bomb or something else?"

Time seemed to slow. His limbs stiffened. He felt as though he was trying to move through molasses. The wailing and crying of the women in his store jolted him back to reality.

"Where are my children!" one of the women screamed. "Are my children or relatives in the street?" Talal opened his front door, still adorned with his daughters' artwork, and peered into the street. The explosion looked to be several hundred meters (one meter is three feet) up the road, judging by the massive plume of gray smoke rising in the distance, close to his home but far enough from where he was standing to not blow out the glass of his storefront.

It was a chaotic scene: "So much smoke. Screaming. Crying." The customers were pressing behind him, the terrified women wanting to check on their families. Talal gently ushered them back inside. "There might be a second bomb," he said. "I know from the news that often a car bomb is followed by another that goes off after people gather at the scene, and it ends up killing more people."

The explosion had knocked out the electricity and disrupted telephone service. Talal and the women—scared, anxious, confused—waited in the dimness of the store for what seemed like an eternity. About five minutes later, they decided that a second blast was unlikely although they had no way of knowing. It was just a guess, a desperate hope intensified by their rising fears to check on friends and families.

Talal stepped into the street and, together with the women, headed toward the scene of the blast. The car bomb had exploded near a bakery close to Talal's home. "I felt like I was on another planet, like I'd been transported to some other place," he said. The street, so familiar, suddenly looked unrecognizable. Thick gray smoke hung in the air. Bursts of bright orange fireballs leapt from the debris. Fire trucks tried to move up the street, but their path was impeded by the piles of gray rubble that minutes earlier had been homes and stores. The private interior of people's homes, their clothes, dishes, and other items, were strewn in the street, near the twisted metal skeletons of several charred cars. A woman rushed past Talal, asking about her son.

"My son! My son! I don't know where he is," she yelled to anyone who would listen.

The sound of gushing water from ruptured pipes spewed a muddy waterfall of muck down the sloping main street. Talal tried with difficulty to navigate the "water mixed with torn tree branches, bits of electricity cables, and chunks of concrete" to reach his home. Broken glass crunched under his feet. He made his way through the crowd of people that had gathered, as residents emerged, dazed and frightened, from their homes and stores, wondering what had happened, who was hurt, and how to help. As he got closer to his house, Talal heard some of his neighbors crying and screaming— their teenage son was badly wounded and covered in bright red blood. He was carried to an ambulance farther down the street.

Talal tried to process the scene: "My house looked so strange, the scene was otherworldly. All the doors had been blown off their hinges, the windows all shattered by the force of the explosion. All around me, there were people screaming, crying, others trying to light the scene with their mobile phones because the electricity was out. Everybody looked lost. I felt as if I was transported back to some earlier century; it was dark, and frightening, I was terrified, and this dirty water was rushing down the street. I was in a state of hysteria." The only thing that calmed him, that somewhat soothed his mind, was the fact that his wife and children were still in Blouta. "All I could think of was thank God they are not here, thank God they weren't in the house when this happened; they may have died in the explosion, or been scared to death."

The November car bomb in Mezzeh 86 killed eleven people and wounded dozens of others. In addition to his teenage neighbor, another of Talal's friends, a nurse, was wounded and lost her leg. A jeweler he knew, a man in his early seventies, was killed immediately. Talal cried for his friends and worried about how the news would reach his family. "I knew that my wife always kept the television on to follow the news, especially at that time when things were getting worse. Her eyes were always on the news, and reports of rockets landing in Damascus. After I saw the destruction of the house, I tried to call but the cell phone network was cut."

Panic set in. He didn't want his wife, Awatif, and his children to hear about the explosion, about the dead and the wounded, in breaking news reports on television and wonder if he had been killed or hurt. He hurried on foot to a friend's house in another neighborhood, all the while dialing Awatif's number until it finally connected. His wife hadn't yet seen the news.

"There's been an explosion in Mezzeh 86," he told her, "but don't worry, I'm okay. The blast was near the bakery, but there isn't a lot of damage, just a few broken windows in our house."

He kept the true extent of destruction from her. "I didn't want to frighten her, so I downplayed the damage. I didn't want her to worry, or to increase her fear."

Hanin heard about the blast from her mother. She burst out crying when she realized that her neighborhood had been targeted. The explosion made the nightly news, but the sisters didn't want to watch the footage.

They couldn't stand to see their neighborhood in such a sorry state.

"When I heard what had happened, I was very afraid for Baba," Hanin said. "It was the first time I'd heard about an explosion in Syria. I was afraid for my country and what was happening, but I didn't understand or know the details. After the explosion, the only thing I was concerned about was checking on Baba. I'd call him every day and ask him, 'Did something happen today? Are you okay?' The only thing I cared about was checking on Baba. I didn't know or try to find out about what was happening in Syria, just in my house and to my family."

Talal walked back to a Mezzeh 86 that felt gray and downcast. The initial shock of residents soon turned to anger and outrage. Some of those gathered around the bomb site began shouting slogans in defiance and pledging their allegiance to President Bashar al-Assad. A chant rose along with the smoke of the still-smoldering wreckage: "With our souls and with our blood, we will sacrifice for you, Bashar!" Talal feared that the car bomb was just the beginning and that there was more trouble ahead.

The war, which until then had felt as if it was happening elsewhere despite the occasional rocket attacks on Mezzeh 86, had now penetrated the heart of his neighborhood. He made a decision—his family would not return to Damascus. They would stay in Blouta. *The village*, he thought, *has to be safer.*

RUHA

Ruha didn't like being stuck in the cellar, with its thick stone walls and arched ceiling, the oldest part of their family complex, but she hated the basement more. At least the room they called the cellar was above-ground. The basement was the family's new go-to refuge when Assad's warplanes screamed overhead and things crashed around them. That was most days now, and more than a few nights. On the worst nights, the family slept down there, in a space crowded with neighbors, aunts, and cousins. There was little safety beyond the illusion of it, only solidarity in numbers. The women of the family had swept the dusty space clean, pushed its knickknacks against a wall, and placed a pile of thin mattresses in the center of its uneven concrete floor. The men had installed a toilet and a kitchenette. Ruha's grandmother Zahida, proud and stubborn, refused to "cower like a rat" in the basement. If she was going to die, she'd often say, she'd die in her bed or on her faded blue couch.

Ruha wished she could stay with her grandmother, but she wasn't allowed to. She wasn't good at sitting still, not for hours that ran into days. She felt suffocated in the airless underground room. "What if it is shelled and we are stuck under rubble?" she asked one day. "At least outside or aboveground we might have a chance to get out, to get away or something, but underground? And under rubble underground? We'll die for sure. Isn't that true?"

Ruha's sister Alaa didn't mind the basement as much. She was calmer and more solitary by nature, but the sudden change in atmospherics would frighten her. "The air, something happens to it, I feel like I am dying," she said. She was too young to know that explosions could suck the air out of a room but not too young to feel it.

The girls had learned the vocabulary of war, new words like *katiba* (battalion), *qannas* (sniper), *hawen* (mortar), *shazaya* (shrapnel). They knew the sounds that accompanied some of the words and how to tell them apart. They fashioned new games from the new words.

They made paper planes, pretend planes to shoot down the real ones above them, to imagine they weren't powerless and stuck in an underground space their parents pretended was safe.

Their mother would hush them, promise them sweets if they were quiet. War or no war, Manal didn't want her girls thought of as ill-behaved. She was more or less raising the children on her own.

Maysaara had pulled away from his family. He wanted his children to get used to living without him, in case one day they had to if he were killed. He also stayed away from them because, he said, "Children can make a man weak. They make a man a coward. I try to keep them at a distance from my heart, from my eyes. It is negatively affecting the children, I know it is, but we have a duty. We're talking about the fate of a country."

He was still helping to finance a Free Syrian Army group comprised mainly of relatives, as well as smuggling medical supplies and satellite communication devices from Turkey. The devices were illegal in Syria, and medical supplies were needed because hospitals were often targeted in regime air strikes. Maysaara transported the goods in black duffel bags he and his nephews carried on their backs across the mountainous Turkish border into Syria. He would pour the jumble of medical packaging in a heap on the basement floor for Ruha and Alaa, their mother, and Aunts Mariam and Noora to sort through. The women placed like with like, creating piles on the floor: packs of gauze, blood bags, intubation tubes, sachets of hemostatic agents, and other items whose use they didn't know.

Manal feared what the war was doing to her children. "They are used to the sound of rockets, it doesn't scare them," she said. "I don't know if it's because they don't understand the consequences of the sound, that if a rocket lands near us, we would, God forbid, die or be chopped to pieces," she said. "They don't understand this."

Except they did. Alaa had even devised a game around it, one she played in the basement. She explained the rules one day. "I hear what they're saying about who died. I memorize it as if I'm recording it on paper. I record it in my mind. I count who died, who has lived, who has left." When asked why, she just shrugged and repeated a word that was her default answer to what was happening around her: "It's normal."

Alaa's other game, the one she played with her older

sister when they were allowed aboveground, was collecting *shazaya*, shrapnel. "Some children collect coins or toys or Barbies; we collect shrapnel instead," Ruha said. "They are like my toys," Alaa added. "I like them, they are unusual shapes."

Alaa displayed the shrapnel on windowsills until Manal scolded her, afraid of the sharp edges and the possibility of explosive residue in the remnants. The sisters gathered the pieces in a plastic bag they hid on the stairwell leading to their flat roof. Another game involved pretending to man a checkpoint and asking passersby for identification. "Are you with the revolution or against it?" a child asked as he stood at his front door. The local version of cops and robbers was now *thuwar* (revolutionaries) and *shabiha* (regime thugs). Nobody wanted to be the *shabiha*. As far as Ruha was concerned, revolutionaries versus regime thugs wasn't a game: "It was reality, something that happened to us and in front of us."

Once, she and Alaa were sitting on the stairs when the house behind them was hit by a rocket. "Mama was drinking a glass of water, I could see her inside; she threw it and started running toward us. We were fine, nothing happened to us, but Mama was about to faint. I was worried she might collapse or something."

"We started thinking of it [bombings] as nothing. Normal," Alaa said. "It was like a game. A bit of noise."

But for Ruha, there was one thing that terrified her more than any other: The open-air inner courtyard where she used to play had become her great fear. She'd dash across it, whispering prayers under her breath, certain the sniper a few streets away and the ones she imagined nearby could see her. The family's rooftop water tank was shot, so she knew her house was within range. She also knew that being a little girl was no protection. The sniper at the old radio communications tower near her cousin Lama's house had shot another little girl in the back, severing her spinal cord and leaving her paralyzed. Her name was Diana, and Maysaara had helped her get to a hospital in Turkey. Ruha saw a photo of the girl in a hospital bed, so she knew it was true, not just something her parents told her when she complained that she wasn't allowed to play in the street anymore.

In Saraqeb, there were new neighbors as parks became

cemeteries and the dead moved closer to the living because existing graveyards were either full or too far away and dangerous to reach during shelling. A growing number of Syrians displaced by violence in other parts of the country had sought refuge in Saraqeb because it was safer than what they were fleeing. Ruha's aunt Mariam cleared out her blackened, burned apartment and allowed a displaced family to squat in it.

The adults, like the children, were trying to figure out the new rules. Assad's hold over towns like Saraqeb had disintegrated, but its replacement was unclear. Criminals exploited the instability across rebel-held northern Syria, kidnapping people for ransom and carjacking civilian vehicles. In the chaos, every man with a gun was becoming an authority. Ruha's uncle Mohammad was carjacked twice in one month at fake Free Syrian Army checkpoints. They took his cars at gunpoint. He accepted the loss of his first vehicle (he refused to pay the 400,000 Syrian pounds, about $6,225 in those days, that the criminals demanded), but not the second. Within ten days of its being stolen, Maysaara retrieved the second car, "by force of guns, not kind words," as Uncle Mohammad put it.

Syria's revolutionaries wanted to bring down the Baathist regime of Bashar al-Assad but not the Syrian state. They didn't want a repeat of Iraq's experience after the US invasion of 2003 and the fall of Iraqi leader Saddam Hussein. In 2003, Iraq's new American overlords dissolved the Iraqi army and every state institution, both civilian and security, as part of their sweeping purge of Baath Party members. At the time, Iraq and Syria were ruled by different branches of the Baath Party, but membership in the organization didn't necessarily mean that a person believed in its politics or was responsible for oppressing other citizens. Membership was often a prerequisite for anything from a government job to a teaching or nursing position to joining a sports club—in other words, nothing more than a box that needed to be ticked on an application. In Iraq, the US-led expulsion of Baath Party members from state institutions left the country without anyone to police it (except the Americans and their allies) or to maintain or repair basic services like electricity and water. The Americans, in dissolving the Iraqi army, made hundreds of thousands of trained soldiers newly unemployed and very angry. Militia violence quickly filled the governance and security void, fueled by anger at the lack of services and jobs and other frustrations of the occupation.

The lessons of post-2003 Iraq loomed large in rebel-held Syria. Revolutionaries wondered how to untangle and dissect the Syrian regime from institutions that over almost fifty years of Assad rule had become a reflection of its corruption and paranoia. Was it enough to remove senior officials and leave the rest? How much of an institution could be hollowed out and replaced without sacrificing people who were competent and knew how to run things for politics? And how to bring the various armed rebel groups under new civilian Syrian opposition control (an impossibility but still a hope)?

Every town in rebel-held Syria struggled with the same questions. Each one had become like an independent island, responsible for its own governance. Communities need rules and laws to function, boundaries that delineate a citizen's rights and responsibilities, and the consequences of breaching them. It's difficult to feel safe and secure if nobody is enforcing the law, or worse if there is no law, and criminals can operate without fear of punishment or being held accountable. To avoid such chaos, in rebel areas where the state's dominance had disappeared, older, more traditional forms of power like religion and tribal authority, once repressed by the Assads, rebounded to fill the governance void. Islamic, or Sharia, courts emerged to try and impose order on lawlessness. The groups of activists known as Local Coordination Committees became the main seeds of budding town and village-level governance systems based on friendships, local reputations, and the size of one's family or tribe. Islamist battalions that were not part of the Free Syrian Army, like Jabhat al-Nusra, also stepped in to fill the void and tried to win over civilians by providing social services that often competed with those provided by the LCCs. In Saraqeb, Jabhat al-Nusra occasionally distributed food aid, bread, and free fuel, and it established its own Sharia court to resolve disputes and punish alleged criminals. It slowly, carefully tried to present itself as a better, more efficient alternative to the LCCs. But Jabhat al-Nusra was not simply a powerful group trying to reestablish order for the good of the people. It was an ultraconservative Islamist militia that did not believe in a secular Syria. It believed that Syria should be governed by Jabhat al-Nusra's strict interpretation of Islamic law, and that God's laws, not legislation created by people, served as the blueprint for society.

Although the majority of Syrians, about 70 percent of them, were Sunni Muslim, it didn't mean they were Islamists. Islam is a religion, while Islamism is a political ideology like socialism or capitalism or any other political theory. The two words, *Islam* and *Islamism*, sound similar but their meanings are different. Muslims like Ruha's family prayed daily and celebrated religious holidays, their women dressed modestly and covered their hair, but they were not Islamists. They did not think multiethnic, multireligious Syria should be governed by Islamic law, and especially not the extremist interpretation of groups like Jabhat al-Nusra. They believed in a civil state where religion was a private, personal affair. Ruha's family supported their town's Local Coordination Committee, even though it had flaws. To Maysaara and his brother Mohammad, the LCC was still better than the Islamist alternative.

Saraqeb's LCC had all sorts of problems, including the corruption of some of its members, and feuds between a handful of the town's key families. The LCC relied on donations, mainly from Syrians in the diaspora, to fund its activities, but the money was inconsistent. One month, it was ten million Syrian pounds. The month before that, only one million. It was hard to plan services and food aid with such irregular funding.

A restructuring of Saraqeb's LCC was proposed. The body's nine elected positions would increase to forty-five, to include representatives from all of the main families—to spread the responsibility and accountability and to expand the body's activities. On a warm summer night, Maysaara and Uncle Mohammad hosted a meeting in their cellar to discuss the new plan. Current and former members of the LCC, the town's notables, and Free Syrian Army fighters were in attendance. But the meeting soon exposed some of the many cracks within the opposition, like the rift between an older generation that was used to being respected and in control, and young people who blamed their elders for not having challenged the Assads earlier. Ruha's uncle Mohammad opened the meeting by saying he resented being told what to do by younger members of the LCC in a society where elders make decisions.

"What did your generation do for us against the regime?" one of the younger men asked. "We fought it, you didn't. You can't tell us what to do now! How many people over forty-five are involved in the revolution?"

Not many, Uncle Mohammad said, because they had family responsibilities. "It's not like we told Maysaara not to get involved. We are three brothers. If something happens to us all, what happens to the family?"

"If everybody thinks, 'I have family responsibilities,' nobody would have moved," the young man countered.

"That's our problem!" another man said. "We argue with each other more than work together. Look at the Islamists and their discipline! I don't blame people for thinking they are cleaner than we are."

"The longer it takes, the more extremists there will be," Uncle Mohammad said. "There weren't armed foreigners in Syria before, now there are. If only Bashar [al-Assad] had introduced reforms, it would have been okay. I'm a democrat, a believer, I pray five times a day, but I'll drink whiskey or beer," he said, meaning that although he was religious, he bent the rules a bit (by drinking alcohol) and was open-minded. "These extremist groups can't dominate Syrian society. We are the majority; our way of thinking will prevail."

"When we finish with Bashar, we may need to get rid

of them," a former LCC member said of the non-FSA Islamist groups. "Even if the regime falls, the harder battle will be forming a new country. We will sacrifice a lot more to create a new country than we will to bring down the regime."

"I don't accept, even now, that Syrians are killing each other," Maysaara said quietly.

"Didn't I tell you that you're not suited to be a military commander?" his brother teased.

Maysaara nodded. "We want a new Syria," he said. "They've tried to kill me many times. I hope I'll get to see it."

Ruha and her sister Alaa may have seemed to their mother a little too unafraid, but their baby sister, three-year-old Tala, wasn't. She was sick with a strange hormonal imbalance that one of the few doctors left in town said was precipitated by fear. Tala was literally scared sick by the war. The toddler needed to see a specialist, but there weren't any nearby—they had either escaped or been killed. There were endocrinologists in government-held areas, but crossing from rebel- to regime-held Syria, especially for somebody like

Maysaara, who was wanted by the government, was even more dangerous and difficult than crossing an official border between states. Turkey was an easier option, but how to get there? Idlib Province, where they lived, bordered Turkey. There were four ways a Syrian could enter Turkey: with a passport, medically evacuated if he or she was bleeding and in an ambulance, approaching border guards and being sent directly to a refugee camp, or illegally smuggled in. Ruha's family didn't have passports. Maysaara said he couldn't bear to put his wife and children in a refugee camp, to see his family living on handouts in tents. They really had only one option—to smuggle themselves across the border. Maysaara told his older daughters to pack for two weeks.

"We're going to Turkey! We're going to Turkey!" Ruha shouted as the sisters hugged and jumped in their coral-pink bedroom. They'd never been to another country. Ruha put more hair clips and bracelets than clothes in her purple backpack. Alaa picked two of her favorite outfits and a selection of T-shirts and shorts. She folded them neatly into her pink schoolbag and then stood in front of the closet full of teddy bears. "Which one should I take?" she asked Ruha.

"What for? We'll be back soon."

Alaa nodded and shut the closet door. Their brother, Mohammad, was just as excited as they were. His sisters laughed when he walked into their bedroom with his blue schoolbag and showed them what he'd packed. "He's put his dirty clothes in there!" Ruha said.

"It's my bag, I can take whatever I want!" he answered.

"Fine. Get in trouble," Alaa said, but neither of the sisters told on him.

The house was full of aunts and cousins who saw the family off, but it didn't feel like Mother's Day to Ruha. "When will I see them again?" she asked. "Do you think we'll leave before the nighttime shelling?"

Maysaara pulled away from the curb a little after 8 p.m. Ruha cried and waved to her aunts and cousins standing outside their front door, until they faded from view. A pickup truck mounted with a 14.5mm anti-aircraft gun moved ahead of Maysaara for protection, and also because one of its two passengers, Maysaara's nephew, was going to drive the family sedan back home.

Young boys cheered, "God salute the Free Army!" as the truck passed.

"We're the Free Army?" Alaa giggled.

Little Mohammad fell asleep in the back seat. Tala clapped to revolutionary songs playing through a USB device.

> Paradise, paradise, paradise.
> Our homeland is paradise!
> Beloved homeland, your soil is sweet,
> even your fire is paradise.

They passed towns that looked deserted, saw garbage as proof of life. In one place, children too young to remember parks and swings and slides climbed miniature hills of rubble where nothing grew, their little hands and shoes coated in a fine gray dust. Streets of disemboweled apartments, barely an exterior door or window untouched by weaponry. A bedroom wall peeled open like a dollhouse, revealing its private interior. The mirror of an almond-colored dresser dusty but not cracked. In another town, a field of stalls—vegetables in purples and oranges and reds and greens. Shoes of different sizes in neat rows along the pavement. "Look, it's normal life," Alaa said. "Is this an opposition [town], too?"

They wove between ribbons of asphalt and dirt roads to stay on rebel-held tracts. They entered an olive grove.

Maysaara slammed on the brakes and turned off the headlights. He'd noticed tank treads in the soft earth. The question was, regime or rebel? The pickup truck had detoured. They were alone. Ruha prayed quietly. "I'm scared," she whispered. Regime or rebel treads? Were there government forces nearby? Maysaara relayed the question over a walkie-talkie to Free Syrian Army units in the vicinity. The answer was inconclusive. There were two routes out, a voice crackled—a shorter one laced with army snipers or a much longer one with a few checkpoints to skirt. Both were dangerous. Maysaara wondered what to do.

"Baba," Ruha whispered, "do we want the easier road or the safer one? Take the safer one. We don't want to be caught and beaten."

Without a word, Maysaara and Manal turned and looked at their ten-year-old and then at each other. "As you wish, madam," said Maysaara. He took the longer route. The pickup truck was waiting for them near the Turkish border. Mohammad woke as the family piled into its back seat.

"Is this Turkey?" Mohammad asked.

"No, we've gone back to Saraqeb," Alaa teased.

They drove to a line of tall trees; then it was on foot from there with a jumble of schoolbags and backpacks. Coiled razor wire glinted in the moonlight. There were silhouetted individuals ahead with plastic bags that rustled, giving them away and prompting commands from the border guards, shouted in Turkish. The silhouettes recoiled. Ruha and her family watched and waited. Somebody approached the wire. Shots were fired into the air, military camouflage came into view. "It's blocked," whispered Maysaara. The family retreated. The pickup truck had gone. Maysaara called a smuggler, and the family waited in the dark until he arrived. They all squeezed into the smuggler's car. "It's a bad night," said the smuggler. "The Turks have moods and tonight they're not blind."

"Does this town get shelled, too?" Ruha asked. It blurred past. Another point along the border. Shots fired. No way across. It was already past midnight. Back in the smuggler's car to another jumping-off point that looked promising. The family stepped onto the uneven ground of plowed fields, the ridges and troughs tricky to navigate in complete darkness. Maysaara walked ahead, carrying Tala and several bags. The smuggler lifted

Mohammad over his shoulder. Alaa shrieked as she fell into a muddy irrigation ditch.

"Shh!" Ruha told her sister as she landed in the ditch, too. "Don't even breathe!"

Wet up to their waists in brown sludge. Manal's black robe caught on the coiled metal teeth of the barbed razor wire marking the border. She took it off to free herself. Still kilometers to the Turkish road and a waiting car. Streetlights beckoned along the horizon.

"Border guards!" the smuggler said. "Into the cornfield!" The family hid in the adjacent field, waiting, resting, then moving, the tall stalks hiding their approach. Rustling. Others were there, too. A Syrian man crashed into Alaa. The little girl screamed.

Maysaara ran to her. "I'm here, I'm here, we're almost there," he whispered. She clamped her hand over her mouth to prevent herself from screaming again, but she couldn't stop shaking. Nobody moved. Had the border guards heard Alaa?

"That's it, we're caught," Ruha whispered. She wanted to go home. She'd had enough of Turkey already. It was too hard to get into.

Waiting in the cornfield. The smuggler made calls. A

group of people had been caught sneaking a large ship-
ment of drugs into Turkey. That's why the guards were
on higher alert, he said, and why they weren't letting
people in. Maysaara carried both Alaa and Tala. Several
Syrian men, strangers, helped with the family's bags.
The cornfield ended and a clearing began.

"Run!" the smuggler said as he stayed behind. Little
legs moved as fast as they could. Manal brought up the
rear to make sure all her children were in front of her.
An old sedan, driven by the smuggler's partner in Turkey,
came into sight. Its engine sputtered, its fumes nauseat-
ing. The family bundled into the back seat as it rattled
toward the nearest Turkish town, Reyhanli. That was as
far as the smuggler would take them. Then, it was a taxi
ride to the Turkish city of Antakya, to an apartment that
housed several injured Free Syrian Army fighters from
Saraqeb, who were in Turkey for treatment.

The two younger children fell asleep immediately.
Turkey that first night was a cramped room with two
mattresses and a couch. Ruha and Alaa changed out of
their mud-caked clothes and collapsed on one of the mattresses. They fell asleep as refugees.

HANIN

Lojayn, Hanin, and Jawa weren't exactly thrilled to learn that their parents had decided to keep them in Blouta. They all much preferred the hustle and bustle of their neighborhood in Damascus. There wasn't much to do in the village, or at least much that the trio of city girls wanted to do.

In Blouta, the days seemed to stretch forever, the pace of life slow and repetitive. Hanin was especially bored. There weren't many children her age to make friends with, and the village school was tiny, nothing like her class in the capital. In Blouta, there were only four students in Hanin's grade.

"There was nobody to have fun with, to play with, and if I wanted to play somewhere, there weren't parks or playgrounds, just the fields full of dirt and mud," she said.

Jawa adapted a little better to Blouta, mainly because several of her cousins in the village were closer to her age. She still preferred Damascus, but she appreciated the beauty of the village, and the rolling hills and deep valleys surrounding it. When she wasn't in school, she liked to spend her time running through the fields with her cousins. "The scenery was so beautiful," she said. "I liked playing, eating figs, planting things, and riding my bike." She and Hanin shared a yellow bike that they kept in the house in Blouta. There was more space to ride it in the village than in their cramped hilly neighborhood back in Damascus. Even Hanin conceded that that was one positive thing about being in Blouta.

Hanin and Lojayn had brought their instruments with them. In the village, with its widely spaced homes, Hanin didn't have to worry about practicing too loudly and annoying the neighbors, because the closest neighbors weren't exactly close. "I'd play my keyboard all the time, all day," she said, "and we also had a lot of toys in the house."

In some ways, being in Blouta felt like an extended

summer vacation, except that their father, Talal, wasn't with them. The girls missed him and wished he'd join them instead of staying in Damascus. He'd drive up from Damascus at least once a month to spend a few days with his family, but he couldn't afford to stay more than that. His daughters always complained when he said he needed to leave, but he never told them the truth about why he had to return to the capital—that business was bad and money was becoming a problem.

"I used to make gross 20,000 Syrian pounds [about $400 before the war], now it's about 3,000 [$50]," Talal once said. His family's apple orchard in the village, a source of additional income, was now off-limits because it was very close to a village called Doreen that was controlled by armed Syrian rebels. Entering the orchard meant risking being shot by the rebels. "We can't go there, we can't benefit from our orchard," Talal said. "That would have helped us financially, but now earnings from our land are nonexistent, so there's no income."

The deteriorating economic and security situation drove more of Talal's neighbors in Mezzeh 86 to volunteer to join the NDF and other security forces, just for a paycheck, but Talal said he couldn't do that. "I didn't want to volunteer and become a killer, but we are in a state of war. There is not a family that doesn't have somebody who is either a soldier or working in the capital or a volunteer militiaman these days [to make money]. Who is staying in the villages? The young and the old, and a few men who work in the fields, but most men aren't there. There's nobody in Blouta except a few old men, women, and children."

The anti-Assad rebels had already taken many of the towns and villages in the Latakian countryside in the patch of territory that extended from the Turkish border all the way to the village of Doreen. Doreen and a nearby town called Salma were the two closest rebel areas bordering regime-held territory in Latakia. Both rebel villages weren't far from Blouta.

The rebels knew that if Assad lost the chunk of territory known as the Sahel, he lost the war just as surely as if he lost the capital, Damascus, because it formed his support base, so the rebels had strong motivation to push deeper into Latakia. Blouta was part of the Sahel, and so, too, was Assad's hometown of Qardaha.

Hanin and Jawa could hear and see the planes flying over their village on their way to rebel areas. They would cheer when the metallic birds streaked across the sky, not realizing they were warplanes on deadly missions. "We didn't know that they were going to bomb other Syrians," Hanin said.

Most of the villages in the Sahel were majority Alawite, not Sunni Muslim like the rest of Syria, and Lojayn, Hanin, and Jawa sometimes heard some of the adults in Blouta whisper fears about what might happen to them as Alawites if the Sunni rebels, especially the ultraconservative religious ones who were saying ugly things about Alawites, tried to enter the Sahel. But other adults, including Talal and his wife, Awatif, weren't worried. They had faith in the Syrian security forces stationed on hilltops around Blouta to protect them. "I didn't have any inkling," Talal said, "not even one in a million, that anything would happen to my family up there."

He was wrong.

RUHA

In Turkey, there was no gunfire or nighttime shelling. No snipers real or imagined for Ruha to fear. She could play in the street again outside her temporary home, a fourth-floor walk-up the family shared with wounded Free Syrian Army relatives from Saraqeb. In Turkey, the parks were still playgrounds, not new cemeteries. Ruha hadn't been on a swing or a slide for almost two years. Her mother, Manal, would sit on a bench and watch her children laugh and run and play without fear of something falling from the sky and exploding. Fifteen days came and went. Ruha's baby sister, Tala, had pending medical appointments, but away from the war, the toddler's strange hormonal condition seemed to be slowly clearing up on its own. Turkey's playgrounds were nice, but they weren't home. Ruha kept asking Baba when they would return to Saraqeb. She cried when she learned they were staying. "We came to treat Tala," Manal told her eldest daughter, "but now the warplanes are as permanent as the birds in the air. We can't take you back to that. We have to try and keep you safe."

"Nobody dies before their time," Ruha replied. Submitting to God's will was a ready-made phrase intrinsic to her Muslim faith and her best argument for going back. It didn't work on her parents. She'd cry when she spoke over Skype with her aunt Mariam, her grandmother Zahida, Uncle Mohammad and his wife, Noora. Her father, Maysaara, had bought the relatives in Saraqeb a satellite internet device. It was their only connection to the world outside their war zone. Their landline coverage did not extend beyond the limits of Idlib Province, disconnecting them from the rest of Syria, and the regular internet had been cut for years.

Mother's Day 2013 was difficult for Ruha. It was usually her favorite day of the year. "We'd make sweets, give my grandmother gifts, we'd all play," she remembered. "I love my grandmother. I know that I'm spoiled, that she spoiled me. When will I see her again?"

The sisters often reminisced about their family in Syria. "Each one of us had a favorite uncle," Ruha once said. "Mine was Ayham, Alaa's was Manhal."

"And I had them all!" little Tala replied.

In Turkey, all the children developed a new habit. At bedtime now, the lights had to stay on. They feared being in the kind of pitch-black of that cornfield the night they sneaked across the border. Ruha and her siblings spent their days watching cartoons on an old laptop, or with crayons and coloring books. They made friends with the Turkish children in their building. They couldn't converse, but somehow they understood one another the way children often do. Maysaara didn't enroll them in school. "How can I put my children in school, as if life is normal, when there are children in Syria who can't go to school?" he said. "My children are no better than those in Syria." It was his form of survivor's guilt.

Ruha was happy not to be in school, but the apartment was cramped with the recuperating Free Syrian Army fighters. The young men were often edgy, impatient to heal and return to the battlefield. "These guys bore me," Ruha would say. "They sit in front of their computers all day, following the news."

Her mother recognized that the young fighters were "emotionally very tired," as she put it. She didn't want her children disturbing them, so she sometimes confined Ruha and her siblings all day to one of the apartment's two bedrooms. "The children cannot speak, yell, cry, run; some of the guys get agitated," Manal said. "I try to keep them quiet, but this is a form of pressure on the children." For Ruha, it was suffocating, like being stuck in the basement back in Syria but without the fear. She wasn't good at sitting still.

They were refugees now, but business-class refugees because they had money. They weren't forced to live in a tent or a converted shipping container in one of Turkey's many refugee camps, unable to come and go without Turkish permission, reliant on food handouts and communal bathrooms, and surrounded by strangers from other parts of Syria. They didn't have to work like other Syrian children, selling packs of tissues or bottles of water or begging in Turkey's streets. They weren't reduced to a pair of hands in a sweatshop factory, paid a few dollars to toil from morning till night, six days a week.

Ruha's parents had enough savings to afford rent and

food in Turkey, but Maysaara was always away as though at work, busy helping other families, with little time for his own. Manal was again raising the children alone. When Maysaara wasn't sneaking into Syria—which was often—to bring in medical supplies, communication equipment such as satellite internet, and donations from wealthy members of Saraqeb's diaspora, he was visiting his hometown's wounded in Turkey's hospitals.

One day he was busy sourcing a large quantity of flour and trying to figure out how to get it across the Turkish border. "The people need bread," he said. "The bakeries have all been hit [by warplanes]. The women will bake, but they need flour." He called representatives of the Syrian political opposition in exile, the so-called leaders who claimed to represent Assad's opponents, and pleaded for money or their help with the Turkish border authorities. "Our political opposition is like, what can I call them? They don't care, they don't ask!" he said. "They're too busy at their conferences! They want to go to Doha and other world capitals, they should go to hell! There's a war and people are focusing on conferences, on YouTube videos advertising themselves. What about the people inside?" After several days, with the help of

Turkish friends, he managed to get a truckload of flour over the border, paid for by donations from Syrians in the diaspora. The political opposition did not help him.

Ruha's parents turned their apartment into a halfway home for anyone from Saraqeb who needed a place to stay—for those who had accompanied wounded loved ones to Turkish hospitals, or recent refugees unsure how to navigate their new life in a new country with a new language. Ruha took heart from the visits. "It makes me feel like I am a little closer to home," she said, "even if the people visiting us from Saraqeb aren't related to us." For her mother, the guests and their stories had the opposite effect. They compounded her survivor's guilt. "We are physically here but mentally there, worried about family and friends," she said. "This is not normal life. It is not normal to live alone in isolation, away from your family and community, to live in limbo. We are living a half-life, permanently unsettled, unstable, temporary." It affected all of her decisions—from whether or not to buy furniture ("What for? We're going back soon") to how her children spent their days ("They'll go to school in Syria. We will return").

It was the knowing what was happening in Syria, the

not knowing, the wondering. Air strikes on Saraqeb meant people would be wounded, some of whom would try and make it to Turkey. Maysaara was often told of impending arrivals by activists in his hometown. He'd rush to the border to meet the injured and accompany them in the ambulance, or he'd wait for them in the hospitals. It wasn't unusual to see people staying in their apartment who were discharged from Turkish care but still too weak to cross the border back to Syria. Manal would cook for everyone. One day, Ruha walked into the living room to see a man with a ghastly lower-leg wound lying on the couch as her father changed his bloody bandages and cleaned the injury. She didn't look away. "If, God forbid, you are wounded," the man told Maysaara, "I will not let anyone clean your wounds except me."

"Brother," another man in the living room said, "the line in front of you is long."

Ruha was eleven now, and she understood why her father was rarely home, and why he seemed preoccupied when he was. "Baba has to do it," she said. "He has to help. Do you think that the people who left their studies and their country wanted to? What does your country, your home, your street mean to you? That's what it means to me. Would you like to leave the home you grew up in? Your family? Who wants to leave those things? If we knew we wouldn't die if we stayed in our home, we wouldn't have left Syria."

Aunt Mariam rattled a small canister of diesel. It was almost empty. She'd been waiting all winter for free supplies promised to the townsfolk by either the Islamist Jabhat al-Nusra or Saraqeb's Local Coordination Committee, both groups competing to provide services and win the hearts and minds of locals. Mariam couldn't be sure and didn't much care which group had made the pledge. She just needed heating fuel. It cost 150 Syrian pounds a liter, as much as 200 pounds in some places—it used to be 25. She poured the thick liquid into the *sobya* heater by flashlight. There was no electricity, as usual. It came for only two hours a day now, shortening the already-abbreviated winter light. Ruha's grandmother Zahida had gone to bed soon after sunset, as she often did that winter. There was no point freezing in the dark.

The *sobya* slowly drew out the dampness from the air. Mariam was in her mother's living room with several of her sisters, nieces, and grandnieces. The women rested on thin mattresses and cushions placed around the perimeter of the room. "Do you know the joke about the genie in the lamp?" one of Mariam's nieces asked. "A man found a lamp, rubbed it, and summoned its genie. 'Your wish is my command,' the genie told the man. 'Great,' the man said. 'I need a bottle of cooking gas.' The next day, the man rubbed the lamp again, summoning an irate genie. 'What do you want?' the genie asked. 'I've run out of diesel,' the man said. 'Couldn't you have waited a few days?' the genie replied. 'Now I've lost my spot in the queue for the cooking gas!'"

Laughter warmed the room. Most of the women had stopped using gas cookers. Firewood was cheaper. Meat was a luxury. Vegetables were more than triple their old price, even after adjusting for currency inflation. The Syrian pound had plunged in value and was so unstable that the currency rate changed daily, sometimes even hourly. Water shortages were common because of the lack of electricity to pump the groundwater. "What can we do except laugh?" one of Mariam's older sisters said. "Praise be to God. We are better off than many, but there's no work, no money. I miss greens! I went to the market yesterday, a man was selling okra. I bought a handful just to taste it. That's all I could afford—six hundred fifty pounds a kilo! But at least he priced it in pounds. Nobody talks about pounds anymore because it fluctuates so much; it's all in dollars. Imagine, dollars!"

Another sister complained about the flour shortages. "My granddaughter keeps asking for cake, she's used to me baking cakes. Where am I going to get flour?" She'd asked a relative in Turkey to send her four kilos. "I don't care how much it costs," she said, "and I paid for transportation, too." The women reminisced about missing the little things they had all once taken for granted, like flicking a light switch and knowing there'd be electricity, or having enough water to take a shower.

The room was dim, lit by a thin LED strip hooked to a car battery, which bathed the women in a grayish hue, just enough to see one another. Their nightly gatherings had become a ritual—air strikes permitting—like an informal therapy session. One night, they recounted the new revolution-inspired baby names in town. An Arab child was named Azadi, a Kurdish/Iranian word for *freedom*. A baby girl was called Thawra, Arabic for *revolution*. Two of the younger women, Mariam's nieces, said their friends were marrying foreign fighters from Jabhat al-Nusra.

"Why are they doing this?" one of the younger women asked. "We haven't run out of Syrian men yet. Bashar is trying his best, but we still have young men."

One of Maysaara's sisters said a foreign fighter told two of her sons to put out their cigarettes because smoking was a sin. "They just ignored him," their mother said. One of her sons told the fighter, "Who are you to tell me what to do? You are a guest in my country."

"They're fighting here for us," Mariam said. "I won't cover my face for anyone, but who else is helping? At this point, I don't care if the devil intervenes." It was one of her most commonly used phrases. "We just want to finish this. Enough."

Desperation had driven some Syrians to embrace the Islamists, who grew in strength and numbers until they were powerful enough to try and impose their ideas on others. To ultraconservative Islamists like Jabhat al-Nusra, smoking was a sin and alcohol was strictly forbidden. The group expected women to be covered from head to toe, dressed in a loose black cloak called an *abaya*, in headscarves and face veils that left nothing except the eyes exposed. That's not how Syrian Muslim women dressed. Many, like those in Ruha's family, covered their hair, but they also wore jeans and tight shirts, long belted jackets, or colorful long-sleeved ankle-length dresses embellished with diamanté and other adornments.

Many people in the Syrian opposition, including some armed factions of the Free Syrian Army, opposed these strict Islamist ideas and sometimes voiced their disapproval. They eyed the increasing clout of conservative Islamists and feared what they might turn Syria into. "We'll deal with them later," some rebels would often say of the extremists, but for now, the disciplined Islamist fighters were needed to help bring down Bashar al-Assad—the bigger, more immediate common enemy. Beyond that common goal, the various types of Islamists and other rebels didn't agree on much else. Although they were all technically on the same side against Assad, they competed with each other for foreign funding and supplies of weapons and ammunition, for the egos of certain commanders, and for prestige. Battalions like Jabhat al-Nusra and others like it were more organized and disciplined than the often ragtag groups that identified as Free Syrian Army, and frequently seized the upper hand in battles against the regime—as well as other rebel battalions that occasionally took them on—snatching the lion's share of any war spoils after battle.

In 2013, Jabhat al-Nusra, which until then had kept its ties to the global terrorist organization Al-Qaeda hidden, was exposed as an Al-Qaeda group. The secret was publicly revealed because of an internal feud within the militia that split the group. Some members stayed with Jabhat al-Nusra while others joined a new faction, a group known in the West by its acronym ISIS. ISIS and its Iraqi leader, Abu Bakr al-Baghdadi, would soon demonstrate with grisly brutality just how violent and oppressive they were, clashing with rebel groups in the Free Syrian Army, snatching territory from them, and imprisoning and killing their fighters.

Both extremist groups—Jabhat al-Nusra and ISIS—wanted to create a conservative Islamic state in Syria, one where religious minorities like Christians were second-class citizens, and Alawites and others who weren't considered "People of the Book" were even less than that. (The People of the Book are followers of Judaism, Christianity, and Islam.) Some other rebel groups also wanted an Islamic state, but their vision was very different. *Islamism* is an umbrella term that represents a spectrum of views. Some Islamists, including battalions within the Free Syrian Army, wanted Syria to resemble Turkey, a state where religion was important in the private lives of many citizens but wasn't imposed or forced on people. Groups like ISIS, on the other hand, wanted to force their extremist ideas on all Syrians, even on Muslims whose practice of the religion differed from their own. For groups like ISIS and Jabhat al-Nusra, the enemy wasn't just Assad and Syria's religious minorities, it was any Sunni Muslim who disagreed with their views—whether on the rebel side or the regime's—and that included women like Aunt Mariam, who refused to cover their faces and obey the extremists' dress code.

Aunt Mariam's niece Mayada, seated alongside her relatives in Grandmother Zahida's living room one night, said that in her heart she wanted an Islamic state—but not the kind the extremist Islamists talked about. Mayada, a young, strong-willed English literature major, recognized that in Syria, a multiethnic and multisectarian society, any type of Islamic state was unlikely. She believed that an Islamic state would be "more just." Her aunt Sarea, who was just a few years older, snickered at her remarks. She wouldn't live in an Islamic state, Sarea said. Unless that state was modeled on Turkey, it would be an excuse to lock women in their homes.

The women debated the issue for hours. The Muslim holy book, the Quran, was clear on the rights of women and minorities, said Mayada. "Clerics will find a thousand Hadiths [sayings of the Prophet Mohammad] to counter it," Sarea replied. In the end, both women agreed that an Islamic state was not the best option—not because Islam doesn't grant rights to women (it does), but because the male clerics who interpret the religion could not be trusted.

Another of Maysaara's sisters retold the story of how her home and car were damaged when two rockets landed nearby at lunchtime one day. "It felt like the sky was raining fire," she said. A neighbor's young daughter died. A displaced family living a few doors down lost a child, while another of its children was left without upper limbs. "I didn't know where to go," Maysaara's sister said. "To the basement? The glass was shattering. To the bathroom? I could hear the yelling outside and the announcements from the mosque, then my daughter called and said, 'Mama, a [bomb] has landed on my in-laws' house.' I put on my headscarf and ran out to see if I could help. What could I do? Their house was on top of them. People screamed, 'The warplane is coming!' I ran back home. Smoke was everywhere. They retrieved my daughter's in-laws in clumps."

"We're sick of it, we're so sick of it," she said. "My grandson, my darling, he hemorrhaged so much when their front door was blown to pieces. We're scared about his eyes. They're still pulling out shrapnel from his body. Every day, it seems they find something new, he's peppered with it. The warplanes just won't stop! They're always in the air. Don't they take breaks?"

HANIN

Blouta was boring, but at least it was safer than Damascus, where car bombs were occasionally exploding and rockets were indiscriminately landing on homes and schools as well as military positions. Hanin and Jawa knew the rebels weren't far from them, that they were congregated in the nearby villages of Salma and Doreen. They'd heard the adults discussing rumors that many of the armed rebels there weren't even Syrians, that they were mainly hard-core Islamists with Jabhat al-Nusra, ISIS, and other groups. That they were Islamists was frightening enough to the girls, but that there were a large number of foreigners among them, fighting and killing Syrians inside Syria, was even worse. What gave them the right to be in a country that wasn't theirs, and to impose their ideas on Syrians? It was a view that Ruha's family, and others on the rebel side, agreed with.

What the Alawite sisters didn't know—and what would have terrified them if they did—was that many of the foreign fighters were drawn to the area by the prospect of killing Alawites. In Doreen alone, seventy-five men had signed up to be suicide bombers to help push rebel forces deeper into the Alawite heartland, the Sahel. There were foreigners fighting on Assad's side, too: Lebanese from the Hizballah group, Iraqi Shiite militias, Afghan mercenaries, Iranian and Russian military advisers, and later, Russian pilots, but those fighters didn't view Alawites and religious minorities as the enemy. The foreign fighters on the rebel side waited with Syrian fighters in Salma and Doreen, facing the sleepy Alawite villages until August 4, 2013, when, in a predawn raid, they seized eleven Alawite villages—and 106 Alawite women and children.

Jawa couldn't sleep the night she was kidnapped. An odd smell drew the eight-year-old out of her bedroom sometime after 3 a.m. She wasn't sure what it was; it smelled scorched, and she wondered why anyone would burn something outdoors at such an hour.

Jawa watched cartoons in the living room. Her sister Lojayn, also roused by the unidentified smell, joined her after shutting off the gas canister in the kitchen, thinking it had leaked. Their mother, Awatif, woke to drink a glass of water and urged her daughters to go to bed. She was still in the living room when the lights went out, the television darkened, and gunfire erupted outside. "Hurry, gather in the corridor!" Awatif told her children as she scooped up her sleeping son. Hanin was also still asleep, so her mother carried her into the corridor.

Men knocked on the gate outside.

"Who are you?" Awatif asked. Nobody answered. She repeated the question. Again, no answer.

"It was dark, we couldn't see much," Jawa said. The men outside "grabbed something, it sounded like metal, and smashed it against the gate. It opened. They came into the garden." The children heard rustling.

"Mama, let's escape!" Jawa whispered. There was just one window, a small one in a bedroom, that wasn't covered in metal security grills. "Mama, let's go through that window," Jawa said.

Her mother shook her head. "I can't fit, and your older sisters can't fit through it. I don't want to lose you. What if they take you?" Awatif and her children, including Hanin, who was now wide awake, waited in the corridor, terrified, wondering what to do and what would happen next.

The front door burst open, and armed men with scarves covering their faces barged in. Awatif fell to the floor, covering her baby son with her body. Lojayn locked herself in a bathroom, Jawa dove under her bed, while Hanin hid under her parents' bed. The men were in the corridor.

"Kill me but don't harm my children!" Awatif told them.

"If there are children, bring them to me," a man replied.

She didn't respond. It was dark and hard to tell how many men there were. The rebel fighters spread out through the house, shooting at shadows. Awatif panicked. "Okay! Okay! Stop shooting!" she yelled. She called her children to her.

The family was marched onto the verandah. Hanin struggled to walk—she'd been shot and was bleeding. She could feel her warm blood streaking down her leg but couldn't tell exactly where she'd been hit; her whole body seemed to hurt. A rebel tank was outside their home. Gunfire and screaming in the streets. Jawa's mother asked her to go back into the house and get their shoes. She didn't want her children stepping on empty bullet cartridges. Jawa returned with shoes for everyone except her mother.

The men with the guns told the family to join the neighbors and relatives walking in their nightgowns and pajamas toward one of the larger houses in the village. Jawa was terrified of the armed strangers, of the gunfire, of Hanin dying because she was bleeding. She felt guilty that her mother was walking barefoot because she hadn't been able to find her slippers.

They entered a house crowded with neighbors, relatives, and screaming, crying children. The house shook from explosions, and Jawa shook with it. Windows shattered. Jawa could hear gunshots and shelling. A neighbor who was a nurse began treating the wounded, but she had little more than cotton wool and disinfectant. Jawa saw the woman cover a young girl's bloody face with a blanket. She didn't understand that the child was dead. Jawa hid behind her eldest sister, Lojayn. Some rebels had shot children like Hanin while other armed rebels distributed boxes of cookies to quiet the children. A rebel asked Lojayn for coffee.

"How do you take your coffee?" Lojayn asked him.

"It's not to drink," the fighter said, "it's to put on wounds. Bring me the container."

The fighter poured coffee grounds on Hanin's thigh to stem the bleeding. Hanin was too scared and weak to resist before she realized that he was trying to help her. He wrapped the wound with fabric he tore from a curtain. His face was covered. Only two or three of the armed rebels revealed their faces, with bushy beards.

One of the bushy beards stepped out onto the balcony of the house and in a loud, strong voice began proclaiming, *"Allahu Akbar! Allahu Akbar!"* to a shower of gunfire.

A rebel with a walkie-talkie and a Kalashnikov rifle walked into the house. He seemed to be in charge. He told the children to go outside, the women to stay. Jawa walked behind Lojayn, who carried their baby brother.

"Put him down and stay with the women," an armed man told Lojayn.

"He won't be quiet except with me and his eldest sister," Awatif said. "Leave him with me."

"No," the armed man said.

It was left to Jawa to carry her crying baby brother outside and help her sister Hanin, who was leaning on her. She heard the man with the walkie-talkie ask what he should do next. "Keep the women, take the children out," came the screechy response.

"And after that?" the man asked.

"I'll tell you later."

The children were directed toward an Alawite religious shrine not far from the house. It was desecrated. Rebels were still inside, smashing images and wiping their dirty boots on religious texts. Other rebels brought the children jam, chocolate, and cookies before herding them into a truck. Jawa's baby brother sat in her lap, her sister Hanin behind her with several of their cousins. There were bags of bullets at Jawa's feet. She was scared to step on them.

Two girls told the two armed men in the truck that

they wanted to say goodbye to their mothers. "Go and see them for a minute," one man said.

The girls came back crying, their faces blood red. "They're all dead!" screamed Zahra, one of the girls.

"Liar!" Jawa yelled.

"Jawa and Hanin, your mother was shot in the mouth and heart and stomach."

Jawa didn't believe her. "The armed men said they'd let our mothers follow us," she said. "I thought maybe Zahra was saying that just to frighten us. I didn't think it was true, but I wasn't sure." The truck started moving. Hanin, an asthmatic, faded in and out of consciousness. The children whispered among themselves. Whatever happens, they told each other, wherever they take us, we'll stick together.

Talal's life changed with a single sentence. He was asleep in Mezzeh 86, unaware of what had happened in Blouta and the surrounding Alawite villages. His cell phone was set to silent, so he didn't hear the eighteen missed calls attempting to rouse him in the early hours of August 4, 2013. He woke at a quarter to six, just as his brother's wife was calling. She lived in a village near Blouta that the rebels hadn't invaded.

"She said that armed men had entered my village and killed my wife and children and everyone in it," Talal said. "That was how the information first reached me."

Talal's wife, Awatif, had called him just the night before. She had told him that she was worried, that something didn't feel right.

"Don't be scared," Talal had told her, "they've been saying they're going to attack our villages for years now; it's just talk, it's just to scare you. The army is on the top of the hills around us. They won't dare come."

Now he frantically dialed Awatif's cell phone. Somebody answered but didn't speak. Talal heard screams, cries of *Allahu Akbar*, and then the line went dead. He dialed and redialed. The calls were unanswered. He sent text messages. *For God's sake, answer*, he wrote. *Tell me what's going on*. No response. He drove toward his village of Blouta, one of the eleven villages seized by rebels that morning, but he could get no closer than a military checkpoint three kilometers away (not quite two miles). The Syrian army was shelling his hometown, backed by air support from warplanes and helicopter gunships. So much gray smoke that it looked like vertical clouds obscuring the houses.

Talal's panic deepened. He remembered what Awatif had told him: If there was trouble—and she had time—she would hide their children in an attic-like storage space above the kitchen. He pleaded with a soldier at the checkpoint. "'Please, sir, don't let the planes hit my house, there's a 99.99 percent chance my children are still in it,'" Talal recalled telling him. "I don't know if he listened."

The truck stopped; the children were ordered into a nearby house. It was small and dirty. "The injured were on the floor," Jawa said. "There were a lot of injured." Jawa felt the responsibility of caring for Hanin, who was wounded, as well as her baby brother. She wondered whether she'd ever see her father again, and whether her mother and Lojayn really were dead, as those girls had told her. Soon after all of the kidnapped Alawite women and children were transported to that dirty two-room house, Hanin was whisked away by their rebel captors. Jawa wasn't sure where her sister was, or whether she'd return.

Jawa sat in the kitchen of that grimy house, near a bas-
ket of cucumbers, her baby brother in her lap. "It's up to
me now," she told him. "I have to raise you. How am I
going to raise you? It's just you and me now."

One of the kidnapped women overheard her. She
told Jawa that she was a distant relative. "Don't worry,
darling," the woman said, "you're not alone. I will
help you."

RUHA

Ruha's uncle Mohammad and aunt Noora weren't home when the artillery crashed into their upper floor on April 25, 2013, the rocket wounding walls and raining rubble into their courtyard fountain. No one was hurt, but days later, elsewhere in Saraqeb, much nastier weapons claimed more than just concrete.

It was a cloudless day, the sky a bright blue, when the chemical weapons tumbled from a helicopter gunship, white smoke trails mapping their paths to three locations. It happened shortly after the noon call to prayer on April 29. A fifty-two-year-old mother, Mariam Khatib, died after one of the tear-gas–type canisters landed in her garden. An autopsy performed in Turkey under United Nations observation "indicated signatures of previous sarin exposure" in her organs. Sarin is an internationally banned, man-made, colorless, odorless, tasteless liquid used as a military chemical weapon, but some countries like Syria still had stockpiles of it. In addition to the dead mother, seven more victims, all foaming at the mouth, with constricted pupils, nausea, and vomiting (symptoms of sarin poisoning), were treated in Saraqeb with atropine. They recovered.

One of the canisters did not explode. It fell intact in a shallow, muddy pond near several homes. Local civilian activists photographed, measured, and weighed it and then informed senior members of the political opposition in exile, who connected them to the Organisation for the Prohibition of Chemical Weapons (OPCW), a global monitoring body that worked to ensure that chemical weapons weren't used in conflict. It was not the first chemical attack in Syria. There had been three previous ones in various parts of the rebel-held north since August 2012, when then–US president Barack Obama warned that the use of chemical weapons in Syria constituted "a red line" that would prompt the US to retaliate against the perpetrators. The Saraqeb chemical attack would also not be the last. In the years to come, Obama's "red line" would be crossed many times with many more chemical strikes, all believed to have been perpetrated by the Assad regime. The US president's warnings were ignored, and the US did not act on its threat to retaliate.

The OPCW didn't conduct an investigation in Saraqeb or take custody of the unexploded weapon. "They said they couldn't if they didn't pick it up themselves," a civil activist from the town said. "What are we supposed to do with it? After months, they told us to hide it in a cave underground and don't tell anybody that you have a chemical weapon."

The activist, an economics graduate in his twenties, was left to dispose of weaponized sarin. He had no idea whether or not it was still live and dangerous or how to deal with it. He feared its being discovered by rebel groups and used against other Syrians as much as it leaking its contents. On July 18, in the golden hue of dusk, the young man walked up a hill on the outskirts of his hometown, a desolate place populated with little more than rocky outcrops and scattered olive trees. He put down his smartphone but continued recording as he rummaged through his backpack and pulled out a large plastic jar—the type used for homemade pickles—and a ziplocked bag containing the rusted canister. He put the ziplocked device in the jar and then cushioned it with household sponges—yellow, green, and pink. He placed the jar deep inside a tight crevice at the foot of a rock formation, as deep as his arm allowed him, then he piled stone upon stone to conceal its opening. He couldn't believe that he had been left alone to handle a chemical weapon, and that nobody—not the OPCW or other international organizations—had helped.

"We thought that if we reveal the existence of the canister, that would end the regime because of Obama's red line and international laws against chemical weapons use," he said. "I had hope that the time will come and the proof will be ready, here in the cave, but nobody cared." To the activist and many like him, Obama's red line meant nothing. "I was very, very, very shocked—I can't tell you how much," he said. "Nobody cared about us or about international laws and forbidden weapons. It made me want to just wait for a [bomb] to fall on me."

Saraqeb emptied after the chemical attack, but Ruha's relatives stayed in their home. Aunt Mariam sat in her mother's living room one day with a younger sister, exchanging the town's news. It was early May, less than two weeks after the chemical attacks, and the air strikes were as ferocious as ever. One of them had recently killed people and charred their bodies. A man had to be identified by a piece of his shirt. A father lost his wife and four children.

"They say that every night he puts out his children's pajamas, expecting them to come back," Aunt Mariam said, "because the corpses were unidentifiable."

Some of Saraqeb's families fled into the fields around their town. A charity organization distributed tents to them from a bakery still under construction. Ruha's uncle Chady, her mother's twin, was volunteering to help build the bakery. He said the bereaved father turned up there one day, asking for a tent to house a family he no longer had. Nobody had the heart to deny his request.

The shelling, once unpredictable, was now as regular as a television viewing guide. Syrians called it "the nightly schedule." One night, it began a little after eleven thirty with the screech of incoming artillery crashing near Ruha's home. A second, then a third strike, each louder and closer, amplified in a night that was black because of the lack of electricity and otherwise nearly silent in a neighborhood emptied of families.

Hiss, whoosh, boom! 11:40 p.m. Another shell. Aunt

Noora shrieked and, flashlight in hand, led her fourteen-year-old niece Lama (whose house had been next door to the sniper at the old radio communications tower) out of a darkened living room toward the basement. Uncle Mohammad cracked open the front door in case neighbors who hadn't fled, especially those without a basement, sought refuge with them, and then he joined his family downstairs. Grandmother Zahida stayed in her bed—as usual.

Another three rockets just minutes apart. What was the target? Like Uncle Mohammad's house, most of the washed-out, low-slung, flat-roofed concrete homes were already disfigured by earlier attacks. There were no rebel bases among them. Saraqeb's rebels had been firing Grad rockets at regime forces all afternoon from outside the town's limits, along a stretch of highway they'd won months earlier. Were the regime's strikes retaliatory, the family wondered, the word *retaliatory* suggesting a reaction, implying a starting point. What was the starting point for that night's barrage? The Grads? The regime's air and artillery strikes before them? The formation of rebel groups? The decades of corruption and dictatorship that pushed protesters out into the streets?

11:53 p.m. Man-made thunder so close it sounded just above the room. The blast dislodged gray snowflakes from the basement's unpainted ceiling, which floated down onto Uncle Mohammad and Noora, Aunt Mariam, and Lama.

"Dear God!" screamed Noora, covering her ears with her hands.

A television news report about a faraway battle could send her into a panic and her relatives into a fit of amusement at her expense. They'd sweetly chide her and remind her that even children had adapted to the sounds of war. Noora never did. She leaned against a vertical concrete support beam. The glow of several flashlights illuminated particles of dust suspended in the stuffy airlessness of the room. Insects scurried across its untiled floor. The ceiling was about thirteen feet high, the room some four yards underground, a single doorway for an exit, two narrow slits of sturdy glass just below street level—windows that were too small to crawl out of.

Aunt Mariam silently mouthed prayers. Uncle Mohammad held a black walkie-talkie up to his ear, trying to hear screechy rebel messages to figure out what was happening, but the words were muffled, drowned in static and noise. Noora wailed at every crash and thud.

"It's not that bad," Lama repeated, her voice sturdy but her hands shaking. "Remember that night when we stopped counting at a hundred and fifty [strikes]? It's not that bad."

11:55 p.m. Another artillery strike, then mortars and rockets in each of the next two minutes.

"Whose homes are they landing on?" Noora asked. There was no outgoing fire, only incoming—a sound heard with the entire body, not just ears. Limbs and muscles and heart and mind tense as the enraged rocket rushes along its arc. Breaths held. Where will it fall? Passive prey in a basement with only one exit. Luck the only difference between a direct hit and a near miss. The projectile lands. Exhale. Breath shallower, faster. It exploded somewhere else, perhaps on somebody else. Limbs and muscles and heart and mind relax, then tense again. The room echoing and shaking to booms reverberating in chests. The time between shells measured in heartbeats—getting quicker, stronger, melding into a single, terrified throb. *Hiss, whoosh, boom!*

"Maybe we should leave tomorrow," said Noora. "I can't take much more of this! What time should we leave? Five a.m., six a.m.?"

"Don't worry," Mohammad said, gently patting his wife's knee. "Bashar's pilots sleep in. We'll have plenty of time."

"Who is counting?" Lama asked. "How many is that now? It's not that bad. It's not that bad."

Aunt Mariam tried to lighten the mood. "One of my friends has a new washing machine," she said, laughing so hard she could barely get the words out. "She calls it *auto eed, auto ijir* [a hand-and-foot automatic]"—that is, she was washing by hand. Even Noora laughed.

12:05 a.m. A few moments of quiet, then the sound of a car outside. The family listened for the wail of ambulances. There were none. "Thanks be to God," Noora said.

12:17 a.m. The few neighbors still around ventured outside, calling out to one another to make sure everyone was accounted for. Uncle Mohammad yelled back that they were fine. On that night, the strikes tore through empty houses, not flesh and blood.

The family did not escape the next morning. They couldn't leave Zahida behind, and she couldn't—or wouldn't—travel. The next afternoon, at 1:30 p.m., just as a lunch of peas and rice, mint and cucumber salad was being laid out, a warplane screamed overhead. The women prayed loudly, Lama put her shaking hands up to her temples. The jet passed without dropping its bombs. But later that evening, the familiar nightly schedule got under way—a little earlier this time, at 11:11 p.m. The family once again scurried to the basement, accompanied by the hiss, whoosh, and boom of things exploding around them.

"Why isn't anyone helping us?" Noora screamed. "Why doesn't anyone care?"

Saraqeb was hit with twenty-two barrel bombs one day in July. The bombs were improvised explosives packed into water heaters or barrels full of metallic fragments and dropped from Assad's helicopter gunships. They were crude, unguided weapons that fell wherever gravity and the wind took them. One of the barrels exploded at the foot of Ruha's street, demolishing the home of her best friend, Serene, the young Assad supporter Ruha used to walk to school with. Serene's grandfather had invited his children and their children to lunch. Serene was the only survivor. She lost an eye in an attack that claimed fourteen of her relatives. Ruha, far to the north in Turkey, cried for her best friend. The barrel bomb did not respect childhood or even politics. It didn't care that Serene's family members were secretly Assad supporters.

After that attack, Maysaara rushed to Saraqeb and insisted that the family vacate to their farmhouse on the outskirts of town. His mother, Zahida, complained but did not deny her favorite son's request. Maysaara and Uncle Mohammad began building extra rooms and bathrooms in the farmhouse. The family complex was abandoned.

Ruha's parents enrolled their children in school that September, in an overcrowded Syrian-run facility in the Turkish border town of Antakya that offered Arabic-language instruction and Turkish lessons. They could no longer ignore a hard truth—Assad was not about to fall and they were not going home anytime soon.

Ruha cried on the first day of school, but then, she did that every year. "Honestly, it doesn't matter how old I get," she said. "It's a habit." She was almost twelve and happy to be with Syrians her own age. "Now," she said, "I have somebody to talk to, to empty my heart to. To take out my frustration."

The school ran in two shifts, morning and afternoon. The older girls, Ruha and Alaa, didn't get home until 7 p.m.; their younger brother, Mohammad, had the earlier shift. Little Tala, who had recovered from her hormonal disorder, started kindergarten. Manal was happy to see her children regain a sense of normalcy that eluded her. Although still living "a half-life" in two worlds, she was relieved the family in Syria moved to the farmhouse and proud that her twin brother, Chady, was helping build a bakery. She followed news of its construction as closely as she oversaw her children's homework assignments.

In early October, Maysaara surprised Manal and their children with a trip to Syria to celebrate the Muslim Eid al-Adha holiday. Ruha was ecstatic. She shopped for days, picking out gifts for her cousins. They returned home to Saraqeb on October 12. The next day, Uncle Chady was killed in an air strike on the bakery. He was thirty years old. His twin sister was inconsolable. A shy, soft-spoken woman, Manal retreated deeper into herself. Ruha was devastated. "I wanted to see Uncle Chady before he was buried," she said. "They wouldn't let me. I wasn't allowed to go and sit in condolences, either. What do they want to protect me from? This thinking is wrong. A child should learn everything, not be told to go to the next room when adults talk. No! We need to know about the situation we are living in, to understand what is happening, to not be frightened by it."

It was dangerous to stay in Syria, Ruha knew that, but she still threw a tantrum a week later when Maysaara said they were leaving. "When I came back from Syria after that Eid, I started wishing to die," Ruha said. "I didn't want to live in Turkey. I'd rather live in Syria, even if I might die. At least I'd be in my home with my grandmother and family. We die when God wants us to, at a time of his choosing, isn't that right? So what do we think we are running from?"

Back in Turkey, Ruha voluntarily did more of the housework, quieted her siblings, helped cook. Her mother was numbed by grief. "I felt like my siblings' mother after Uncle Chady died," Ruha said.

Maysaara stayed home more. He took Manal and the children on day trips to the beach, to the mountains, to the mall as often as he could, but none of it seemed to draw his wife out of her deep sadness. Manal struggled with a grief made heavier by its invisibility.

"In the beginning, they used to say the names of the

martyrs," she said, "then the martyrs became numbers. The day Chady died, his name was not mentioned. He was a number, one of thirty-six people who died in Syria that day. Nobody is talking about us as people. On top of the oppression and the war, we are also dehumanized. We are people."

By mid-2013, the United Nations stopped counting Syria's dead due to the difficulty and danger of verifying information. Estimates put the death toll at well over half a million people. Syria had become a conflict where the dead were not merely nameless, reduced to casualty figures—now they were not even numbers.

HANIN

anin had been separated from her siblings, whisked
away by her rebel captors along with two other
wounded children, including her six-year-old
cousin Reema, whose foot was bleeding profusely.
It was dark and the ten-year-old couldn't see where she
was going. The pickup truck mounted with a 12.5mm
antiaircraft gun in the back bounced over bumpy mountain roads.

Hanin's mind was a jumble. What had happened to her
mother and Lojayn? Were they really dead? Were Jawa
and her baby brother in danger of being harmed?

She remembered what the armed men who burst into
her home had said: "Don't be afraid, we don't kill women
and children and the elderly." But then, when they were
all squeezed into their neighbor's house that terrible

night, she heard whispers that one of her uncles in Blouta had been killed. She couldn't get the horrible sound of that night's gunfire out of her head. Were some of her family members killed in that hail of bullets?

It was all so sudden. One minute she was asleep in bed, the next minute she was living a nightmare she couldn't have even imagined. She was terrified in that pickup truck driven by armed rebels, unsure of where they were taking her and what would happen when they arrived. *They're saying they don't kill the elderly or women and children, but they've killed my uncle, an old man,* she thought. *Why did they kill him? Will they kill us, too?*

The pickup truck stopped, and Hanin and the two other children were transferred into a waiting ambulance. The ambulance was a relief to see: "I felt better because I realized they were going to treat us, not kill us. They won't kill any of us."

The ambulance stopped, the doors opened, and a man gently carried Hanin out of the vehicle and into what looked like a partially destroyed residential building surrounded by rubble. It was a medical field clinic.

Makeshift field clinics, many in secret locations, had sprung up across rebel-held northern Syria. Their locations weren't widely advertised (although locals knew where they were) because hospitals and medical facilities were often targeted in regime air strikes. The field clinics were usually poorly stocked, with limited equipment and staff. Destroying a hospital and killing health workers had broad ramifications for local communities—it made it harder for people to survive, not just the wounded but others, with conditions such as diabetes, who required constant care, or children who needed vaccinations.

The field clinic Hanin was brought into was a year old. It was in an otherwise abandoned apartment building in the rebel-held town of Salma. It had four doctors and ten nurses, most of them male, who lived and slept where they worked. There was no running water or electricity in the facility, which relied on diesel-run generators to power medical equipment, including a digital X-ray machine, an ultrasound machine, and a portable ventilator. The clinic, which was funded by US- and UK-based charities, was well stocked, unlike many others that lacked even basics such as anesthesia and bandages. Water came via a pipe that dipped into a spring on higher ground three kilometers away. Months earlier, the six-story building had taken a direct hit—a barrel bomb blew out most of its windows and pancaked the two upper floors, spewing chunks of crushed concrete onto rosebushes below. The pink flowers, however, still bloomed.

Hanin and the two other children were treated for their wounds. Hanin was told that she was in Salma and that the doctor and his staff had removed a bullet from her left buttock. They were very attentive to her and the other captives. One nurse in particular, a woman who told her that she had a daughter named Hanin, was especially kind to her. "She liked me a lot and I liked her," Hanin said. "She'd bring me food, and bring me whatever I wanted."

Hanin was soon back in the ambulance. It had been five days since she was shot in that dawn raid. A rebel handed Hanin a cell phone and told her to call her father. She called the landline in Damascus. Her father picked up.

Talal's heart leapt when he heard Hanin's voice. It was the first contact he'd had with his family since the raid. Hanin told her father that her siblings and mother were with her, because that's what one of the rebels told her to say.

"Where are you?" Talal asked his daughter.

"In Aunty's lap."

"Which aunty?"

"Aunty Ghada."

She didn't have an Aunty Ghada.

A man with a Syrian accent took the phone from Hanin. He told Talal that his wife and other children were dead. "You only have her left," he said. "If you want her, go to Latakia and tell the head of the Military Security branch (one of the four main intelligence agencies) to negotiate with us. We won't speak to anyone else." The men holding the 106 Alawite women and children wanted a prisoner exchange with the regime.

Hanin knew the rebel was lying because Jawa and their baby brother were with her, or at least, they had been until a few days ago. Had something happened to them? Were they killed? Was this rebel telling the truth and she was the only surviving member of her family?

The phone line died. Talal wondered what to do. He was confused and terrified that the rebel's words might be true—that only Hanin had survived. He contacted relatives and other people from Blouta whose families were kidnapped and shared the rebel's message about the prisoner swap. Talal, along with other families, tried and failed to get an audience with Latakia's head of Military Security. They saw his deputy, who brushed off their concerns. They approached other officials. The head of the local Baath Party chapter offered to arm the families.

"He said, 'We will protect you, we will arm you.' I said, 'After what? After the gangs entered the area, killed who they killed, kidnapped who they kidnapped?' I was shaking, crying, screaming."

The governor of Latakia asked the families what the armed men wanted. "He was asking me!" Talal said. "If a dog is lost in Europe, they set up an operations room to find it. I told him, 'Am I supposed to tell you the news?'" Talal left the meetings angry and dejected. "They don't feel with us," he said. "They're officials who are just there like a framed photo. We mean nothing to them."

The only things Talal was sure of were that one of his children, Hanin, was alive, because she'd called him, and that he'd fallen between two fires—rebels who viewed him as an extension of the regime just because he was an Alawite like President Assad, and a regime that didn't seem interested in helping him. Blouta didn't receive special government attention because it was Alawite, he said. "Our villages were neglected, poor. We have unemployment, too. I swear to God, I carried a bag on my back for three years and went from pharmacy to pharmacy and to hairdressers selling cosmetics and perfume. I worked as a night guard, as a construction laborer. Why didn't they [the rebels] think that some of us have problems, too?" He ruled out approaching the Syrian political opposition for help. "It's impossible," he said, "because these members of the opposition, whoever they are, are killers and partners in the deaths or kidnappings of our children—without exception." Talal viewed the opposition the way many fighters on the other side of the Latakia front viewed him. Nuance was lost as each side's position hardened.

On August 12, 2013, the first images of the Alawite captives were released in a three-minute, eleven-second video uploaded to YouTube. They showed the women and children seated along the perimeter of a roofed outdoor area, in the presence of an armed guard whose face was covered by a balaclava. Talal saw his three youngest children among them but not his wife or eldest daughter, Lojayn. The man on the phone had lied to him. Hanin wasn't the only survivor. Over the next month, the same captor called Talal four times, demanding a ransom of four million Syrian pounds (about $35,400 at the time). Talal didn't have that kind of money. He asked about his wife. The captor said she was dead. Talal didn't believe him. He asked for proof of some kind, a photograph or to know where her body was buried, although he still hoped that the news wasn't true.

"Do you think your wife is the only one who died?" the captor said. "Many women died."

Hanin returned to the grimy house where the detained Alawite women and children were being held. Hanin and Jawa were overwhelmed with relief to see each other. Jawa was surprised by how well Hanin looked and how she'd been treated in the field clinic.

"She was wearing new pajamas, her hair was combed and tied, her nails were cut and painted with polish. They looked after her the way Mama might have looked after her," said Jawa. It lessened her fear a little. The male doctor and a female nurse later checked on Hanin and the other wounded captives. Jawa thought the man had a kind face. His name, she recalled, was Dr. Rami.

Dr. Rami was a forty-three-year-old Sunni Muslim from Latakia. He didn't care that the captives were Alawite. As far as he was concerned, he was a doctor and they were wounded, and it was his duty to treat everybody, even if some Syrians were demonizing other Syrians who were different from them. A Syrian-trained physician, Dr. Rami was in the United Kingdom to specialize in pediatrics when the Syrian revolution began in March 2011. He returned to Latakia soon after to check on his elderly parents and never left. He knew his services were needed in Syria more than anywhere else, even if his wife still lived in the United Kingdom.

"I told her I have to do this, and she accepted it," he said. "Of course without her support I couldn't have done it—peacefully," he added, laughing. "Someone has to do it, right?" He spent all his days and nights in the field clinic in Salma.

One day, not long after Hanin had been treated there, a shout came from the rubble-strewn street outside his field clinic. "It's one of the Alawites! It's one of the Alawites!" a man yelled. Dr. Rami heard the cry through the sandbagged window of his dark basement office. He ran toward the nine-bed, street-level emergency room.

A little girl, one of the Alawite prisoners, was carried in by her captor, a foreign fighter, and carefully set on a sapphire-blue plastic sheet covering a bed.

The child was Talal's niece, six-year-old Reema. She was back in the clinic less than two weeks after she'd first been treated there with Hanin.

"Uncle, please don't hurt me!" she said as the doctor reached for her bandaged left foot. Her bloodied dressings were stained brown. She wore clean, three-quarter-length pink leggings and a pink T-shirt. Her hair was short, her brown bangs swept up into a tiny ponytail that sprouted from her head like a mushroom.

"Don't be scared. We need to change these bandages," Dr. Rami said.

"Uncle, it hurts a lot," she cried. "I'm scared."

A warplane roared overhead before the doctor could reach for a pair of scissors. Rebel antiaircraft fire thundered from several positions around the clinic. The little girl screamed. Her captor, who was unarmed except for a knife, patted her ponytail while another doctor fetched a packet of cookies and offered her one. Reema declined the cookie. An explosion outside. The little girl was now wailing, interspersing her screams with "Uncle! Uncle! Uncle!"

Several of her toes were dark brown. Large sections of skin on the top of her foot had sloughed off, revealing red-raw flesh that bled. Dr. Rami changed her dressing and took aside the young jihadi fighter who had brought her in. A jihadi group of foreign fighters named the Battalion of Emigrants was holding the prisoners. "Tell your emir [leader] that I say hello and that this girl needs to go to a hospital because her wounds must be cleaned under general anesthetic," the doctor said. The foreign fighter nodded, swept up the child, and left.

Dr. Rami was pained to see children—on all sides— paying a price in this grown-ups' war. He'd treated more children than he could count who'd been wounded in regime air strikes, and he wasn't happy about the Alawite children being kidnapped and harmed. "Detainees, innocent people, should be treated well," he said. "These women and children are not enemies; an enemy is who- ever is carrying weapons against us and wants to kill us. Children are innocent. These children [the captives] are like our children."

Dr. Rami returned to his small office—or control room, as he called it—and sat on one of the thin mattresses around its perimeter. A 10.5mm handgun in a brown holster was tucked into the space between the mattress and the wall. A TV sat in one corner, near two walkie-talkies set up to interact with the other field clinic in Salma.

"I miss normal life," said the doctor. "I miss watching a movie." He reached for a pack of cigarettes. There was an explosion outside that tossed bits of rubble into the room through the glassless window. Two minutes later, another explosion shook the room.

"Emergency!" The call came from the street above. Dr. Rami rushed to intercept the casualty, a Syrian fighter hit by a large piece of shrapnel, his legs barely attached to his torso. The fighter died soon after he arrived.

Throughout the night, men moved in and out of the control room with requests for Dr. Rami—some wanted help finding accommodation for a Free Syrian Army group, others needed stocks to replenish frontline first-aid kits and supplies for a midwife. A father, clutching his daughter's hand, wanted to have his child vaccinated, but Dr. Rami said vaccines weren't available in "liberated Syria," only in regime-held areas where the Health Ministry functioned, and from international aid organizations that dealt only with governments. In "liberated Syria," as he called it, or rebel-held Syria, hospitals were targets for regime air strikes, not government vaccination programs. A local farmer walked in with a bag of fresh green beans he donated to the clinic.

"Plane in the air!" somebody yelled from the hallway. Ten minutes later, an explosion outside. It didn't take long for the familiar call to come from the rubble-strewn street: "Emergency!"

Two men lay on the sapphire-blue plastic sheets covering the beds—a Syrian with shrapnel in his left foot and a foreign fighter from Chechnya with two bullets in his right leg. The Chechen had been brought in by several of his countrymen. They were all dressed the same—green skullcaps on their shaved heads, T-shirts, and loose pants so short they rode halfway up their shins. "What brought you here?" one of the Syrian nurses asked the wounded Chechen.

"We came for God's name," he replied in formal, stilted Arabic.

Both men were treated and sent to better-supplied clinics farther north, away from the front and closer to Turkey. Dr. Rami returned to his control room. He'd tended to about thirty fighters and almost as many civilians that day.

"You know what we forgot to do today?" said Dr. Rami to a colleague reclining on a thin mattress. "Send the tractor to dig more graves. We'll need about ten by tomorrow, and then another twenty or thirty."

The colleague nodded. "Yes, we forgot to do that."

The doctor lit up another cigarette. "It's a slow day today, thank God," he said. Outside, the sounds of explosions continued, near and far.

By August 19, two weeks after the eleven Alawite villages were captured, the regime regained all of them. Two days later, Talal drove to his hometown of Blouta. He saw burned and ransacked homes, including his own, and a mass grave with human remains. Syrian soldiers in fluorescent-orange vests placed bodies in bags, including two of Talal's brothers and his father. Talal had no information about his wife and children or what had happened to them. The rebel perpetrators left behind graffiti on schools and homes that identified them. *Jabhat al-Nusra will bring victory to the people of Syria* was spray-painted on one wall. The raid had been spearheaded by ISIS and a group of mainly foreign fighters named Suqoor el Ezz. Units of the Free Syrian Army were also there, but not in the lead.

Syrian state media reported mass graves in two of the eleven Alawite villages but didn't specify the number of dead, beyond stating that there were dozens. On October 10, the international organization Human Rights Watch put the figure at 190 killed, most on August 4, including at least 57 women, 18 children, and 14 elderly men, in "incidents that amount to war crimes."

Talal snapped pictures on his cell phone of his burned home, the rebel graffiti, the mass grave. He shared it with another father, a man named Abdel-Hady, whose family had also been kidnapped from another village, and together the fathers lamented what had happened and what they could possibly do. The rebels "want to place the crimes of the regime on the shoulders of our [Alawite] sect," Abdel-Hady said. "They say we are still with the regime, that we haven't split from it. Who is going to defect from the regime and join an opposition that stands under a black Islamic banner? It's impossible. To be an Alawite to them is to be a germ."

"I am certain that Syrians can live together again," Talal replied. "I know men from Salma, I know that not all of them are happy with the armed rebel groups. Anybody who clings to the idea of Syria as one nation, not a Syria of sects, is in danger of death—not just us, the Alawites, but the Christians and moderate Sunnis, too."

"There are *shabiha*, Alawites, who have committed crimes against Sunnis for being Sunnis," Abdel-Hady said, "and they have also harassed us because we are against them. The extremists in the opposition have also harassed moderate Sunni civilians who do not agree with them, as well as us. So the issue is political, it's about interests. We understand this, we want the regime to leave but will its removal guarantee us our safety? I have my doubts. I want the regime, the head of the regime, to fall, but not the Syrian state. I don't want the institutions of the state to crumble."

It was a view that many Syrians on the rebel side, including Ruha's family, understood and agreed with.

RUHA

Ruha's little sister Tala, whose illness was the reason the family fled to Turkey, couldn't remember Syria. She'd forgotten the warplanes and barrel bombs and mortars that had scared her sick, couldn't recall details of her home or the harrowing trip across the border. Perhaps that's why she seemed to her mother the best adjusted of the children. It was late 2014, and they'd been refugees for two years—a long time in the life of a five-year-old. Tala had reverted, physically and emotionally, to being a normal little girl again, one unburdened by memory.

Ruha envied her that. Some days she wanted to forget, too; other days she clung to the memories, the good ones, wrapped herself in them like a life jacket. "I can't forget Syria," Ruha said, "but I want to forget what I saw in Syria, because it's ugly. I want to forget especially when Baba was shot. I try very hard, but I can't. The past was difficult. No matter how much I try, I can't forget."

She had a new baby brother, Ibrahim, born that summer, who drew his mother out of her grief. Ruha was twelve now, and like many Muslim girls entering puberty, she had taken to wearing a headscarf. It was her choice to do so. It made her feel grown up.

She was still attending the Syrian school in Antakya with her sister Alaa. Her brother Mohammad had transferred to an all-boys' Turkish school nearby. His classmates called him Mehmet, the Turkish version of his name, which his sisters teased him about, but he didn't mind. He'd laugh along with them. The children were learning Turkish at school, and they took pride in the new words they'd memorized. "Now at school," Alaa said one day, "we are studying history and geography. In history we are talking about things that happened a long time ago."

"When we study history and geography," Ruha replied, "I tell the teacher, 'Why are you telling us about things that happened so far in the past? We are living history now. Isn't that enough?'"

Ruha preferred to look forward, not back. She had started contemplating her future. "I'm thinking I want to be a doctor, a pediatrician to help other children. What subjects do I have to take to be a doctor?" she asked. "I want to return to Syria. I want to rebuild my country, take our rights. I think of Syria every day, but it's getting less. I don't think about my house as much anymore. I wonder sometimes and I feel guilty that my house is still standing and others aren't." Saraqeb, she said, was her life, "my other life, the real one."

Her father, Maysaara, didn't tell her that the house in Saraqeb was so damaged it was unlivable. Their family in Syria had moved permanently to the farmhouse. Friends and relatives who had land around town did the same.

Ruha's aunt Mariam still visited the old neighborhood from time to time. She didn't like going there but felt drawn to it. "I go, cry, and come back," Mariam said. "There's so much rubble, so many destroyed homes." Aunt Mariam still taught at a local primary school. The schools in Saraqeb also ran in two shifts, because buildings were either destroyed by war or were bases for armed groups, including Jabhat al-Nusra, the Al-Qaeda affiliate.

"Four or five schools have started using one school building now," Aunt Mariam said.

Because of the planes in the air, the teachers had reduced the curriculum and eliminated sports, music, and art classes to minimize the time students spent in schools.

One day, there were two air strikes while Mariam was teaching. "The children were scared. I told them not to be, that it was a friendly plane and it wouldn't hit us." The older children, she said, were the ones who cried and screamed, not the younger ones, "maybe because the [younger ones] were born into this environment, they don't know anything else."

Aunt Mariam was teaching, running a household, and taking care of the business of the farm. Her brother, Ruha's uncle Mohammad, was ill; in June 2015, he died of stomach cancer. Aunt Mariam rented portions of the family's vast farmland to people who could grow crops and work it. She scoffed at the idea of leaving Syria, even temporarily. "Leave?" she said. "And go where? I won't go anywhere! I will die on our land. There is no place that I'd even think of going. Not one!"

That summer, Maysaara, like hundreds of thousands of Syrians, contemplated risking Turkish waters to reach Europe and a new life. The Syrian war had precipitated what the United Nations called the worst refugee crisis since World War II. Half of Syria's twenty-three million people had been forced from their homes and displaced either internally or externally, beyond Syria's borders. Some sought safety with friends and relatives in other parts of Syria, or in wretched camps for the internally displaced, while others, like Ruha's family, escaped to the neighboring states of Turkey, Lebanon, Jordan, and even Iraq. Millions of extended families like Ruha's were now living apart, separated by borders between states or internal borders within Syria that defined communities as either pro- or antigovernment. Conditions in Syria's neighboring states—which had absorbed millions of Syrians and borne the overwhelming burden of the refugee influx—were difficult for Syrians, and getting worse.

In Lebanon, there were so many Syrian refugees that,

at one point, every fourth person was a Syrian. There were no formal refugee camps in the country, so Syrians had to rent apartments or even the land they pitched their tents on, in a country that was many times more expensive than Syria and had a tortured history with its much larger neighbor.

For decades, until 2005, Syria had dominated Lebanon, and many Lebanese had not forgotten or forgiven, and they scapegoated Syrian refugees for all of Lebanon's many woes. Lebanon was a country with poor infrastructure, with daily electricity cuts and water mismanagement, and the addition of more than a million Syrians further strained basic services. The government refused to establish formal refugee camps because it feared that they would become permanent—like the twelve Palestinian refugee camps scattered throughout Lebanon that were established in 1948 and 1967 and still existed.

Water-starved Jordan, one of the driest countries in the world, was also sharing its scarce resources with more people. It set up camps, including the sprawling Zaatari refugee camp in northwestern Jordan, which in 2013 housed 120,000 of the half million Syrians who'd fled to Jordan. The refugee camp was the second-largest in the world, so massive that it was basically Jordan's fourth-largest city. It was located in an arid, otherwise forgotten patch of desert that was little more than scorpions and sand before refugees were housed there. For Syrians, used to the greenness of home and Syria's abundant water, the adjustment to life in an isolated desert camp, with its common toilets and kitchens, disease and over-crowding, was very difficult.

In Turkey, too, despite its many refugee camps and the free food, education, and shelter the facilities provided, life was becoming harder for Syrians, who found them-selves caught in internal Turkish political rivalries, with some Turkish parties supporting the continued presence of Syrians and others demanding they return to their war-torn country. Syrians like Ruha's family who weren't in the camps weren't immune to these pressures and faced the additional economic burden of supporting themselves.

As for Iraq, it was once again embroiled in war, this time against the extremist ISIS group that was active there as well as in Syria. ISIS had carved out what it called a caliphate, or an Islamic state, in the Syrian city of Raqqa and its surroundings, a territory that extended across the border into Iraq and included the city of Mosul. ISIS imposed its harsh rules on Syrians and Iraqis living in its so-called caliphate. It carried out countless atrocities, destroyed cultural heritage, forced women to be completely covered in a loose black abaya, headscarf, and face veil, and did not permit females to travel, even to the store, without a male guardian who was a close relative. ISIS publicly punished anyone who opposed it or whom it deemed an enemy. The punishments were grisly and included floggings and beheadings. Many Iraqis, especially those in areas that ISIS was trying to push into, were fleeing their country; it wasn't even safe enough for them, let alone the Syrian refugees who were streaming in, fleeing their own war.

And so, in 2014 and 2015, many Syrian refugees in Turkey and elsewhere looked to Europe as a way to escape the pressures they faced in Syria's neighboring states. More than a million people would eventually arrive in the European Union. Many, many others would drown trying to get there.

Ruha's father, Maysaara, considered escaping to Europe. In 2015, he traveled to the Turkish coastal city of Mersin and looked out onto a calm sea, the serenity of the water disguising its bloodlust. Its dangers had been demonstrated many times in refugee boats that capsized, drowning dreams and belching corpses. Many Syrians, entire families, had died trying to cross these same waters to reach Europe.

Smugglers offered passage in boats that were nothing more than rubber dinghies. The smugglers operated openly, doing business in cafés in Mersin and other Turkish coastal cities. Besides the latest fashions, store mannequins in these coastal towns also displayed bright orange life vests.

Refugees mapped out their trips and exchanged advice on Facebook pages and WhatsApp groups. They slept in cheap hotels or on the streets, waiting their turn to leave. Maysaara watched a family, not unlike his, haggling with a smuggler. The smuggler insisted he wasn't like others who overfilled their rubber dinghies, making them unsafe, that he had a conscience. The parents listened and walked away. They couldn't afford the premium for a conscience. Maysaara stood outside a smuggler's office one night, wondering what to do. He'd been in Syria twenty days earlier for about a week and said it was worse than ever. His words tumbled out, as if he needed to hear them, to convince himself.

"There's no more hope," he said. "Now it's clear this isn't going to end anytime soon. Everybody's trying to figure out what to do, how to live, where to live, how to survive. It's gone on for too long. There aren't many of us left, the ones who started it, who aren't dead or detained. These new commanders, these new defectors, are something different. They want to tell you about our history! Where were they during that period? There are a million things in my head and I don't know what to do, which path to take. All the guys are saying that, at the end of the day, we should leave the country. How can we leave? Leave our homes? Leave our lands? Leave it to whom? I'm in Turkey, but I still feel like I'm close to Syria, that I can get to it when I need to. Europe is a different kind of exile. If I lose Syria, I lose everything. If you leave it, you don't deserve to return. People died for it. We paid in blood. What am I if I leave? What will I become?"

Maysaara didn't get on a boat. His memories, heavy and rich and painful and proud, weighed him down. He returned to Antakya, bade farewell to his wife and children, and crossed into Syria alone. He sold a piece of land for enough money to live comfortably in any of Syria's neighboring states, but that wasn't his plan. On September 19, 2015, he sent a photo of a pile of metal he'd just bought, and room-size holes dug into cinnamon-colored earth that would soon be filled with concrete. He planned to build a factory to process the land's bounty in Saraqeb and to provide employment for his community.

"This is our land and our country," he said. "Our land is our honor, it is our past and, God willing, our future."

HANIN

The Alawite prisoners had been moved again, this time to a ground-level apartment. Their new prison had a little terrace where the children could play and the women could hang laundry. They had been in so many different places. There was their first jail—a dirty two-room house for 106 people, with one blocked toilet that overflowed. They stayed there for a few weeks before being woken at night by the armed rebels.

"They said, 'Get up, get up,'" Jawa remembered. "They put us in a truck. We were squashed sitting on top of each other. They said, 'Not a sound, don't speak. We're taking you to a better place.'"

They were moved to a clean villa with a large kitchen that had electricity via a generator. The wounded, including Hanin, were kept in a separate room and were the only captives allowed to sleep on the few beds and mattresses in the villa. Jawa and her baby brother, like most of the other prisoners, slept on bare tiles. They stayed there for several months before they were moved again, this time to an empty chicken farm that crawled with bugs that scared Jawa. She was glad to be in their current prison, the apartment with the terrace.

Dr. Rami, the doctor from the rebel field clinic in Salma, and his nurses regularly checked on the women and children, supplying them with fresh vegetables, meat, rice, clothes, female sanitary products, and medical attention as required. The Alawite women were given utensils to cook for themselves and the children.

Their days melted into weeks and months in captivity, until May 7, 2014. The captives were told that about half of them would be released as part of a broader prisoner exchange between the rebels and the regime, tied to a cease-fire deal in the Syrian city of Homs.

But there was a catch—prisoners from the same family could not all be released. Somebody had to stay behind, the captors said, to pressure the family members in regime-held territories to force Assad to negotiate their release. The more families represented, the better. Hanin and Jawa were told that two members of their family would be released. Their baby brother was definite, but which sister would go and which one would stay?

"They didn't care which two of us were released," Hanin said. She and Jawa argued over which sister should stay, each wanting the other to leave. They didn't have much time to decide.

Hanin told her two younger siblings to go.

"You're wounded and an asthmatic," Jawa told Hanin. "You should return to Baba with our brother."

"I'm older than you," Hanin told her sister. "I'll stay, you go home. Keep your faith in God and take care of our brother."

The captors were distributing food to the women and children who were to be released, to know whom to load onto the trucks. Hanin handed her juice and cookies to Jawa. "If I get out, I'll have access to everything, you have nothing here," Jawa told her sister. "You drink the juice."

Hanin refused, and Jawa and their baby brother, juice in hand, were ushered into waiting trucks. Hanin watched them walk away, relieved that their ordeal would soon be over. "I couldn't leave one of them behind.

Imagine! It's impossible that I leave my brother or sister and go! I made Jawa leave. I'm older than her, and for sure I can handle more than she can. She is very young and weak, she can't stay alone. I sent Jawa home."

Their father, Talal, like the other relatives of the captives, learned of the prisoner release on May 7, the day it happened. A cousin working in the government hospital in Latakia called him at 1:30 p.m. and told him that the governor had asked to prepare a ward for Alawite hostages on their way who needed to be examined.

"I just assumed it was another lie," Talal said. "All I heard was that some of the detainees were being released. I hoped my wife and children were among them."

Jawa and her baby brother arrived at the Latakia government hospital that afternoon. The little girl cried at the kindness of hospital staff, who brought her and the other freed prisoners cookies, falafel, shawarma sandwiches, French fries. "They kept telling us we were free, we were safe, we would soon be home," Jawa said. "I couldn't believe it, but I worried about Hanin. I wished she had come with us."

It was too late for Talal to travel to Latakia and see his children that day. It was already 4 p.m., and the road from Damascus to Latakia was dangerous at night. He'd have to wait until the next morning. The children's maternal aunt lived in Latakia City, not far from the hospital. The children were discharged into her care.

"My aunt's house was full of people," Jawa recalled. "Aunty couldn't keep up with serving coffee. So many people were there to check on us. My aunt was crying so much she went hoarse, she couldn't speak."

The next morning, Talal left Damascus at 5 a.m. and was in Latakia by 10 a.m. He ran into his sister-in-law's house, screaming out the names of his children. He saw two of them. "They seemed as if they had shrunk, like they were years younger," Talal said. "Jawa was thin. She didn't know me, her words burned me."

Jawa mistook her father for her uncle. "I asked him, 'Where is my father?'" Jawa said. "He was calling out my name, 'Jawa! Jawa!' I thought he was my uncle. He seemed very different to me—older, tired."

Talal realized that his wife and eldest daughter, Lojayn, were probably dead because they weren't among the captives—either those released or those still held. His "heart burned" that Hanin was still in captivity. "Hanin is very special to me," he said. "She has asthma. I used to take her once or twice a month to hospital to have her lungs and sinuses cleared. I imagine her in the dust of battles, of places they are hiding them, the dirt. How is she living there with them?"

RUHA

March 2016. Maysaara hadn't seen his wife and children for more than seven months. He was in Syria and they were in southern Turkey—the days of moving easily between the two countries now as distant as the idea of peace. Sneaking into Turkey was no longer simply a tough hike with the fear of a Turkish jail or deportation to Syria. The once-porous border had tightened since mid-2014, when Turkey, under international pressure to trap the extremists of ISIS and Jabhat al-Nusra in Syria's killing fields, began erecting a concrete barrier of blast walls topped with coiled razor wire, placing it well inside Syrian territory. Some stretches of the border were monitored with thermal cameras. The Turks were shooting dead anyone trying to get across—fighters and refugee families alike—although they sometimes held fire and instead detained and deported those they caught. It wasn't as hard to get into Syria as it was to get out, but the shoot-to-kill policy meant risking death.

Maysaara wanted his family with him. His youngest, Ibrahim, had forgotten him. He called every male relative Baba. Manal feared returning to a Syria that was no better than the one she'd fled, but she didn't want her children growing up without their father. They were going back that summer. Manal walked around her living room one day in March, wondering how to pack up her "half-life" and what dangers were awaiting her and her family. Two families she knew of, sixteen people, were recently obliterated in a farmhouse.

"There is no safe place in Syria, even our farmhouse is not safe," Manal said. "What can I do except try to calm the children and tell them not to be afraid? This is the Syrian woman's burden—caught between worrying about our men and [worrying about] our children."

Her eldest, Ruha, who had pined for Syria, was now a teenager who suddenly didn't want to return. "We are children of now, not children of before," she said one day. She got along with everybody in her school, even though she knew not all of the girls were with the opposition and that some supported Assad. "We joke about it, nobody takes it seriously. We don't really talk about it; the problems aren't our problems, they are with the adults," she said.

Friends and rap music and hairstyles and fashion were displacing thoughts of Saraqeb. She dearly missed her father, but beyond that, she was accustomed to freedoms in Turkey she didn't think she could carry across the border.

Her classes that year were during the school's morning shift. Her afternoons, when she didn't have homework and it wasn't raining, were spent in a park with a diverse group of girls: There was the Chechen born in Turkey whose father was fighting in Syria, a Turk whose mother owned a stationery store across from the park, and a Syrian who always arrived after 4:30 p.m., the end of her day at a sewing factory. Her family needed her wages more than her education. The girls didn't share a language—just a few Turkish words here, Arabic there, lots of sign language and laughter.

Ruha sat on a bench with her sister Alaa one day, waiting for her friends to arrive. She discreetly pointed to a

Syrian woman, in a long, belted overcoat and a face veil, pushing a child on a swing. "Look at my clothes and look at the Syrians here, look how they're dressed," she said. Ruha was in skinny jeans, a long sweater, and a head-scarf, common attire for a Muslim Syrian girl, but she expected to have to dress like the woman in the park if she went back to Saraqeb. She had heard her relatives talking about how it was more conservative now because of the influence of the Islamists. "I have a lot of freedom here," she said. "If I go to Syria, that freedom will be imprisoned. I'll have to wear a coat down to my ankles like that woman. I can't do that."

She was growing up. She didn't want to burden her parents with her concerns. "The family used to sit together at mealtime, talk about our day, but now I feel like everybody is in a different universe," she said. "Now, whatever happens to me, I don't have the courage to tell Baba, to ask him anything. I know he has other things to worry about. I don't tell Mama, either. I prefer to speak to others my age. That's why I come here. We haven't seen Baba in more than seven months. That's wrong. When we were in Syria, in the war, Baba wasn't with us much, but we used to see him occasionally. Even if I saw him for an hour, I felt like that hour was worth the entire world and everything in it. Now . . ." She couldn't finish her sentence.

May 2016. The sun was low in the sky, its golden light soft and warm and diffused. It cast long shadows on the handful of construction workers ending their day. Maysaara watched them climb down from a two-story wooden scaffolding hugging the building's rectangular shell. His factory was coming together. It had four walls and no roof, its exterior built in the traditional manner, with great blocks of locally sourced white stone, not the cheaper concrete. Saraqeb's silhouette rose five kilometers (three miles) in the distance, on the other side of green carpets of shin-high lentil crops and young stalks of wheat. Sprinklers pulsed rhythmically. Deep-orange pomegranate flowers were in bloom. Birds chirped in the quietness when the warplanes weren't overhead.

Maysaara walked through his empty factory, proud and excited, explaining where the equipment would go. The machinery would come either from the regime-held city of Hama (through the forty-nine government checkpoints along the route, each one demanding a bribe) or

from Turkey, with its raft of paperwork and tight restric-
tions at the border. It depended on the roads, the planes,
and the required bribes, but he wasn't overly worried
about it.

The construction site was a short drive from the farmhouse, on land the family had owned for generations.
Maysaara surveyed its sweep, pointing to the plot in the
far distance where a hundred fig trees would soon be
rooted, near the olive groves his late father had planted
decades earlier. He had bought half a dozen sheep and a
puppy his daughter Tala named Molly, after one of her
favorite cartoon characters. He had plans to restart the
family's cucumber pickling business, to give young men
an alternative to emigrating or joining a battalion to
earn $50 a month. And he wanted to buy a horse, recount-
ing a Hadith, or saying of the Prophet Mohammad,
about how those who treat a horse well are blessed against
poverty. He scooped up a handful of earth, let it fall
through his fingers. "This," he said, "is everything. I
swear a person doesn't find himself or feel dignity except
in his own land. I lived in Turkey for three years. I lived
well, was treated well, but I am still a foreigner there. I
mean, the Japanese were hit with nuclear bombs, and they

stayed in their country and didn't give up on it! How can we? Look"—he stretched out his arms—"here, there is life." His Syria had shrunk, he knew that. Regime territory and areas such as the city of Raqqa, which was now controlled by the extremist group ISIS, were like separate countries, but his space was enough for him. "Before the revolution, I wasn't somebody who spent a lot of time on Latakia's coasts. I will sacrifice seeing the sea. This is my land. This is my area. This is my country."

Wasn't he afraid to bring his family back? "Life and death are in God's hands," he said. "Some people survive being in a building hit by a barrel bomb that others die in. It's not their time. Nobody knows when their time is up."

It was getting dark. The workers had long left. Maysaara drove back to the farmhouse in his red Toyota HiLux pickup truck, the same vehicle in which he'd been shot back in January 2012. It had been idle for years while he decided what to do with it. He patched its forty-eight bullet holes and cleared its bloodstains. He refused to sell it. It was a reminder of what he'd survived and what others, like his friend Abu Rabieh, who had died in the front seat, had lost.

Ruha's aunt Mariam was up early the next morning, and so were the warplanes. It was not yet 8 a.m. when the first one roared overhead. Mariam walked into the living room, carrying a tray of Turkish coffee. "Good morning," she said. The bombs tumbled to earth somewhere far enough away not to worry about them. "Who wants coffee?"

A walkie-talkie set near the window screeched out an alert about another warplane: "Sukhoi 27 is coordinating with Homs, be careful." Saraqeb, like every town in the rebel-held north, had developed an early-warning system to identify threats in the air. Men known as *marasid*, or observers, were tasked with intercepting regime communications between pilots and air bases and relaying that information via walkie-talkies. They latched on to regime frequencies that constantly changed and tried to break the coded language sometimes used to identify targets. More often, the targets were simply stated. The planes had few real predators. If the threat to Saraqeb was direct, and there was time, the alert would boom from the minarets of mosques. The town had five *marasid*, their task made harder since September 2015, when Russian warplanes joined their Syrian allies in the skies, turning the conflict decisively in Assad's favor. There were Western planes in the air, too, rebel backers bombing ISIS positions in other parts of Syria and the occasional Jabhat al-Nusra post, but the Western planes didn't target the Assad regime.

Mariam laughed when asked how people without transmitters coped. "Even beggars have walkie-talkies these days," she said.

The farmhouse was self-sufficient, with twenty-four-hour electricity courtesy of solar panels, two generators as backup, satellite internet, and two water wells. Residents who couldn't afford their own generators or solar panels subscribed to private neighborhood generators that distributed electricity for a monthly fee. Cell phone reception was still dead. The landlines worked, but only for local calls within the province.

Aunt Mariam didn't have classes that day. She got behind the wheel of her gray Kia Picanto, said a prayer under her breath, and drove to the market inside Saraqeb. Along the way, she recounted how a member of Jabhat al-Nusra had recently stormed into the school, demanding that religious instruction be expanded and social studies be struck from the curriculum.

"We all debated him," Mariam said, until a compromise was reached: Religious instruction would remain unchanged, social studies would be taught, but all references to the Baath Party, democracy, and socialism would be removed. "We slammed him into the wall with our words until he came out the other end!" Mariam laughed. "We will not be silent to them or anyone anymore."

She had never accepted the growing Islamization of her town. She always drove herself, was politely waved through Islamist checkpoints, and never covered her face with a niqab, although many more women in Saraqeb now did. Ruha was right about that.

"Before, in the beginning, I used to think we have to be frugal, not use too much cooking gas, too much diesel, too much fuel. Now I don't think like that," Mariam said. "Now I don't care if all of my paycheck is spent. We are in a state of war, who cares about money? Why die with money in your pocket? Why not live as comfortably as we can while we can?"

In the beginning, as Aunt Mariam put it, there was one martyrs' cemetery in Saraqeb for those killed in the conflict. Five years later, there were three. On another day, at one of the newer cemeteries, the gravedigger was busy shoveling red earth out of a deep hole. He always prepared ahead. The graves were arranged into sixteen rows, each row extending at least a hundred meters (just over a hundred yards), each column broken by plain white headstones, like rungs on a ladder. Daisies sprouted from the graves. At least twenty belonged to unidentified victims, some placed in the earth just months earlier. The gravedigger explained what happened: "A plane struck, two fuel sellers were hit. Their supplies exploded, killing them and killing people in a Kia Rio that was passing by," he said. "The bodies were charcoal, there was nothing left for us to identify them. Nobody knows who they were or where they were from or going. We put notices on Facebook, but nobody has asked about them." Even the cemeteries weren't safe from the planes, the gravedigger said. Another one in town had been shelled. "The living were martyred and the dead were martyred twice," he said. "Life is the cheapest thing in Syria now."

Aunt Mariam's eldest sister needed cooking pots. Hers were riddled with shrapnel. Mariam offered to take her first to the family complex in the center of Saraqeb to see if there were any left behind, before she bought new ones. The sisters drove around piles of rubble and twisted metal, Mariam cataloguing the lives lost at each gray mound. Four. Fourteen. Twenty-two. Six.

"This was a little store," she said, pointing to a concrete skeleton, the missile's entry point clear. On a surviving column was a message spray-painted in red: *Here there was life.* Two men died there.

Mariam turned into their old street. Her sister waited in the car: "I don't want to see it," she said. "It hurts my heart." Mariam fumbled with the keys to the heavy metal door, its yellow fiberglass paneling long since blown out. It was the same door a once-nine-year-old Ruha opened to security forces back in 2011, the first time they invaded to look for her father.

Mariam's footsteps echoed in the emptiness. The windows, all glassless, were filled in with cinder blocks. Doors blown off hinges, window frames blown out, too. The wind whistled through holes in several walls. A warplane overhead. Washed dishes gathered dust in the kitchen rack. A bottle of olive oil and spice jars on the bench. The inner courtyard, where Ruha and her siblings once played, where Mariam and her sisters would gather in the evenings, was strewn with rubble. In a coral-pink bedroom, dolls and teddy bears waited for two little girls who'd outgrown them. A fourth-grade social studies textbook lay on a bed. Colorful socks in a drawer. A pink desk with two chairs.

Mariam didn't find any pots. "I feel numb when I come here. I say to myself, 'Don't get upset, the whole country has been destroyed.' At least we're all okay, but I always feel tired after coming here, physically worn out."

The old family complex was empty. Life had relocated. Ruha's extended family now gathered at the farmhouse each week, turning every Friday into Mother's Day. The matriarch, Ruha's grandmother Zahida, was frailer, her body confined to a wheelchair but her mind still formidable, the anchor of the family. She expected updates on the crops, the price of lentils, the currency fluctuations, how her thirty-five grandchildren were faring, and what was happening in town.

She sat on a couch one Friday afternoon—a new couch, not the faded blue one that had molded to her shape. Mariam was in the kitchen, preparing lunch with a few of her sisters. The smell of fried onions and bay leaves and spices hung in the air. She made kibbe, a labor-intensive dish of finely ground meat and bulgur, cinnamon, and allspice, fashioned into palm-size, football-shaped croquettes, each one stuffed with minced meat, onions, garlic, and spices. It was a festive food, served in times of celebration. She hadn't made it in five years.

"Why should you die wishing you'd eaten something?" Mariam said. That was reason enough to prepare it.

A male relative walked into the kitchen and joked that Jabhat al-Nusra wouldn't approve of the gender mixing. Islamists preferred that men and women were separated. The family laughed and mocked the Islamist messages.

"They just make people hate them more," a sister said.

"Did you all hear about what Abu Stayf did?" Maysaara asked. The lines outside bakeries were gender-segregated, with armed Nusra guards supervising the distribution. The bakeries were also targets for Assad's warplanes, so women tended to stay away. The men's line was always longer. Abu Stayf, a local man, had wrapped his face in a scarf and stood near a female friend in the shorter line. The Nusra fighter on duty, a foreigner, approached the woman suspiciously, asked her who was standing next to her but wouldn't look directly at her. "This is my sister, but she's hairy," the woman said, referring to Abu Stayf.

The Nusra fighter took her word for it and simply asked, "How many loaves?" when the pair got to the front of the line. Abu Stayf walked away, bread in hand, to applause and chants of *Abu Stayf! Abu Stayf!* "He turned around and made a V-for-victory sign!" Maysaara said, chuckling.

One of Ruha's aunts talked about her detained son. A former prisoner from Saraqeb had been released recently and was expected home soon. Ruha's aunt wondered whether he'd seen her boy behind bars. She was dealing with a middleman who claimed he could release her son, but he demanded tens of thousands of dollars in advance without providing proof of life.

"If he'd only give us something to believe [her son] Abdullah was alive, we'd sell land to raise the money," Ruha's aunt said. Abdullah had been detained on April 21, 2012.

His mother, aunts, cousins, and grandmother remembered him fondly that afternoon, recalled his laugh, and argued about whether he had one dimple or two. "You wonder what they are doing to him, what they've done. God help him," Aunt Mariam whispered. "The mothers of the detained have it much harder than the mothers of the martyrs. My friends, mothers of martyrs, at least they know what happened to their children."

In early July 2016, Ruha and her family returned home. Maysaara met them on the Syrian side of the border and escorted them to a farmhouse full of relatives waiting for them. Despite her earlier misgivings, Ruha was glad to be back, glad to be reunited with family, and pleased to know she didn't have to dress as conservatively as she had feared.

She started school, made new friends. She was a ninth grader now. "Everything has changed," she said of her hometown, "or maybe I'd forgotten the details. It's like I am seeing it for the first time. I wasn't expecting this destruction." She was upset that her home in the grand old family complex was too damaged and dangerous to live in. She also was surprised by how much she'd acclimatized to Turkey, how easily she'd forgotten the fear of life in wartime. "If I want to go to the souq, I have to think about whether it's worth it, think about the warplanes, and make it a quick trip. Even in school, when

I'm in school and a plane passes, I'm terrified. Everybody is. The teachers freak out."

In Turkey, she said, "I felt the exile, the distance, but I also felt safe. I'm happy here with my family, but I got used to safety. *Inshallah* [God willing] the future is better. *Inshallah* we stay united and the fear disappears, because I don't want to have to feel like I need to choose between living with family and being safe. Why can't we have both in Syria? Nobody wants to have to leave their country just to feel secure."

In July 2017, Saraqeb's sons and daughters, including Ruha's family, protested against the armed Islamists with the black flags in their hometown, peacefully driving them out of Saraqeb, although few expected them to stay away. The revolutionary flag fluttered from vacated Islamist outposts, and for the first time in years, a new revolutionary slogan appeared on Saraqeb's walls: *Say to those who try to destroy us that the beauty of our souls cannot be defeated—Saraqeb 2017.*

HANIN

The ambulance was smeared with mud to make it harder for warplanes to see. It bounced along potholed Idlib roads rendered almost impassable by shelling. Dr. Rami was in the front seat, scanning the skies through a bullet-fractured windshield. His field clinic in Salma had been destroyed in Russian air strikes that had helped the regime win back most of Latakia Province as well as other areas.

In September 2015, the Russian Air Force joined its Syrian counterpart in the skies over Syria, and together their warplanes bombed villages in Latakia until they emptied of residents, the survivors fleeing toward the Turkish border. Entire villages in Latakia were displaced and reconstituted in clusters near the Turkish border. The temporary towns were a patchwork of thousands of

tents, some canvas, others simply sheets of plastic or bur-
lap bags sewn together, their occupants hoping the air
strikes that drove them from home wouldn't hunt them
so close to Turkey's blast walls. Dr. Rami had evacuated
as much medical equipment as he could carry. He was
personally financing the building of two hangars to
serve as a new hospital as well as a hundred adjacent
greenhouse-shaped homes, each seven meters by four
meters (about 23 by 13 feet), to shelter some of the displaced. Until the hospital was functional, his team of
fifteen (down from twenty-six) spent their days moving
from camp to camp in the three ambulances they still
had, treating patients as best they could. Dr. Rami's new
hospital, however, would never open. On November 8,
2016, when it was almost ready, its two operating rooms
fully tiled, a regime air strike destroyed it all, including
the homes he was building. Cockpit-view footage of the
strike was broadcast on Syrian state television, lauding
the destruction of "a terrorist military camp" belonging to
foreign fighters. Except, it wasn't a camp; it was a hospital.

But on April 25, 2016, as the mud-caked ambulance
climbed higher into Idlib's green hills, that destruction
was yet to come. Dull thuds, several per minute,

rumbled like distant thunder. The sound of shelling else-where. The ambulance turned into the narrow streets of the once-majority-Christian village of Ghassaniyeh, an area draped in the black flags of an Islamist fighting group. The destination was a village church, its crosses removed by the foreign Islamists. The building now served as a prison for the fifty-four remaining Alawite captives, including Talal's daughter Hanin, now almost three years into their ordeal.

Dr. Rami still periodically checked on the women and children. He was embarrassed by their continued deten-tion. "This is a nightmare. I have nightmares about this," he said. "It's a stain on the revolution, a catastrophe. This crisis is a deep wound, but what I know is that even deep wounds heal."

A unit of the Free Syrian Army called the First Coastal Division guarded the hostages in place of foreign Islamists. The group was not involved in their kidnap-ping, which had been the work of non-FSA conservative Islamist battalions. A pair of armed guards sat in the church's courtyard, drinking yerba mate from a black-ened teapot. They worked twenty-four-hour shifts and were frustrated with their "babysitting" duty.

Jabhat al-Nusra and its allies were still the decision makers. "Their expenses, their security, nobody is helping us," one of the guards said. "Our job isn't to stand here over hostages. We are supposed to be on a front line fighting the enemy, not having guys occupied with this."

His colleague complained that the captives didn't seem to be as valuable as had been hoped. "They're not asking about them," he said, referring to the regime. "They won't negotiate for them. We are surprised."

The women and children had been moved at least six times to escape shelling and other rebel militias trying to steal them. The rebels were so fragmented that they competed for everything, and the prospect of dozens of Alawite prisoners who could potentially be exchanged with the regime, or ransomed, was an attractive prize. The rebels posted outside Hanin's makeshift prison weren't there just to make sure she and the other captives didn't escape: They were mainly there to make sure other rebels didn't take them to try and swap them or, worse, kill them.

"There are hundreds who want to harm them, but we won't let them," one of the guards said. "We will be judged by Almighty God for how we treat them. This duty was imposed on us, but we must protect them. They must stay in our hands. We can't just release them without anything in return. There are thousands of our women in Assad's prisons, and I assure you they are not treated the way these women are. Nobody has touched the Alawites, we don't even look at them. Our women are raped in prison. We want an exchange, women for women, that's it."

The heavy, black-metal gate at the entrance to the church hall was newly installed—the prisoners had been there less than a week. The padlock clicked open. The men stayed outside. The captives sat silently on thin mattresses around the perimeter of the room, twenty women and thirty-four children. They were dressed not in the casual skin-baring fashion of Alawites but in conservative Muslim garb—long robes, headscarves, and niqabs. They hadn't been permitted calls to their families since September 19, seven months earlier. Their captors no longer saw the usefulness of communications meant to pressure the regime to seek their release.

"We are of no value, it seems," said a prisoner named Shaza al-Hatab, who served as the group's spokeswoman. "That was the last we heard, that nobody is responding because we are dogs to the regime." Behind the padlocked door, the women and children were free to move around in a number of rooms, to cook and use the bathrooms at will. They spent their days sewing, teaching the children, and reading the Quran in a bid to impress their captors.

Hanin was wearing an ankle-length, long-sleeved pink dress and gray headscarf. She was now twelve and a half, almost the same age as Ruha. She sat near her thirteen-year-old cousin Sally—quiet, scared, fidgeting, staring at her hands but wanting to talk. Ruha recounted the night three years earlier when she woke to gunfire and strangers in her home in Blouta, the moment a bullet burned her left buttock while she hid under her parents' bed. The wound had left a puckered scar. She remembered what the strangers said when they made her mother and eldest sister, Lojayn, stay behind: "They said our army massacred people in [the Syrian rebel town of] Baniyas and that this was in response to that."

She had heard from those two girls, fellow kidnap victims, who went back into the house, that her mother and sister were dead, but Hanin still wasn't sure. In every one of the five calls she'd been allowed to make in almost three years, she asked Baba where her mother was. "He kept telling me she was with him," she said. Hanin was relieved that her two siblings were free, and she wondered when she'd join them. She wasn't the only child hostage alone without immediate family. There were eleven others, including her cousin Sally, who had sent her three siblings home while she stayed behind. The eleven children were all adopted by women who vowed to care for them until their fate was decided, one way or the other.

"I think about my house, my school, about my siblings," Hanin said. "I think about my future, which has been completely destroyed. I wanted to be a doctor, but it's impossible now that I'll be a doctor."

"Nothing is impossible," one of the women told her.

Hanin had a message for her father, Talal, one she struggled to articulate through tears, pausing often: "Baba, I miss you and my siblings. When are we going to be released? Baba, I miss my school. I miss my freedom." Her voice broke in her throat. "I can't speak. I'm not able to speak."

Talal locked his tiny perfume and cosmetics store in Mezzeh 86, as he did every afternoon for a few hours, crossed the street, and walked up a darkened stairwell to his first-floor apartment. There was no electricity, as usual. He tried to be home before his daughter Jawa and his son arrived from school, but they were already inside when he turned the key. Jawa sat on a mattress in the small lounge, trying to do her English homework by the dim light of an overcast November day.

Talal hadn't heard Hanin's voice in more than a year. He wept as he listened to his daughter's brief taped message. Jawa, dry-eyed and steely, handed her father a tissue. He had knocked on so many doors, he said, heard so many promises from officials who "all sold us pretty words" but seemed to do nothing to free the captives. "They said, 'Our hearts are with you. Your children are our children. Your honor is our honor.' We heard it all, and from all of them. Alawites and others, but we saw nothing in practical terms. Nothing."

Back in 2013, a senior presidential adviser had even publicly claimed that the captured Alawites were all dead, the real victims of an August 21, 2013, chemical attack against the rebel town of Ghouta, an attack the adviser insisted was perpetrated by rebels, not the regime. Talal had followed the news of Christian nuns held hostage by Jabhat al-Nusra and exchanged for Nusra prisoners, of Russians and Iranians swapped for hundreds of opposition fighters. "What about our children from the Latakian countryside?" he said. "Why is it just our case that is in the shadows, that nobody wants to talk about?"

Some of the Alawite families had discussed kidnapping Sunni women and children from Salma and Doreen to force a swap. Talal rejected the idea. "I won't make another family cry," he said, "and I won't seek revenge for my murdered wife and daughter. I hope there is an international resolution to the Syrian crisis; otherwise we will continue living like this, in a cycle of killing and kidnapping. Syria must return to what it was."

If only the men holding his daughter wanted money, he said, he'd try to raise it, but they were asking for something he couldn't do—he couldn't free prisoners. "Why should our women and children pay the price for their victims? We are not responsible for whatever happened to them. We are victims, too. We're not living in paradise over here because we're Alawites," he said. "Our villages are poor. I was in eighth grade before my village got electricity. Municipal water came only in 2010. I'm not saying things were great before, I am neither with the regime nor the opposition, but there had to be a thousand solutions instead of arms, to kill a fellow human just because he's with the regime or opposition."

If he could sell his house in his hometown of Blouta, he would, he said. He hated going to the village, seeing where his wife and eldest daughter were killed. He felt helpless. A widower struggling with the loss of his wife and daughter while trying to raise traumatized children who woke at night screaming. "They're here now and I still have nightmares that they're detained," he said, "that they're being kidnapped. They have nightmares, too. They still do."

The teachers at their school knew what had happened to Jawa and her brother, and were careful to treat them kindly. The first month they were released, they received psychological therapy from a charity organization. "Jawa talks about what happened to her all the time. Every day she repeats the same stories. I let her talk, let her empty her heart, I want her to let it out, maybe it will help her."

Talal kept Hanin's clothes in her closet, her school report cards within easy reach. Hanin's purple slippers were by the door with everyone else's. "Sometimes he just sits and stares at Hanin's slippers for hours," Jawa said. She had turned back to her English homework. The assignment was to recall a special day. She wondered what to write about, then decided on a family trip to the Latakian coast in 2009. A picnic lunch, shells from the shore, sand in her shoes, games in the water. "We were all together. My parents, siblings, cousins. That's what made it a special day."

"We need to forgive each other," Talal said. "That's the only solution to end this. I forgive because nothing will bring back my wife and my daughter Lojayn. Let them know I forgive them, maybe it will help the killers and criminals remember their humanity. Are they able to wash the hate that they have for me out of their hearts? We were neighbors. I used to go to Doreen and Salma whenever I wanted. I have friends from there. How did they suddenly become killers and kidnappers?"

Hanin had heard the promises before. The words were always the same, repeated every few weeks or so by a small group of civilians who recently started bringing the prisoners food and other supplies: "You'll be released soon," they'd say, or "Freedom is near." Hanin didn't believe them. It was easier that way. It hurt less to have no expectations than to get your hopes up only to see them crushed.

The group was not part of Dr. Rami's team. Its members told the captives that they were working to free detainees. Hanin didn't believe that, either. If they really were working to free detainees, she figured, why was she still detained? The group had visited Hanin and the other prisoners several times since late 2016. The Alawite prisoners referred to the men as "the organization." Their identities were unclear beyond that they were pro-opposition. Even the few Alawite activists who were aware of the prisoners' plight and were working with Talal and the other families weren't sure who these pro-opposition people were, beyond their wanting to negotiate a prisoner swap. There were many different groups on the rebel side, both civilian and armed, who claimed to have the Alawite captives or access to them, although most were frauds with no connection whatsoever. These frauds were just trying to squeeze money out of parents like Talal, their lies and false claims an added source of stress for families desperate for news of their detained loved ones.

Hanin had grown used to the organization's empty promises; they were yet another part of her monotonous reality. She and her cousin Sally were starting to think they might never see their families again, until one winter morning in early February 2017, when Hanin woke to the sound of the padlock on the heavy black-metal gate breaking open. Several men rushed into the church that served as Hanin's prison.

"Hurry up! Get dressed!" they shouted. "Quickly, quickly!" They were from the organization.

Hanin threw on her clothes and, still half-asleep, rushed toward the entrance. She ran outside into the vast church courtyard, feeling the early morning chill on her face. The three rebel guards suddenly woke up. The men from the organization outnumbered the rebels, but unlike the rebels, they were unarmed.

Pop! Pop! Pop! Gunshots fired into the air. "Nobody leaves!" one of the rebels yelled.

"Leave!" one of the men from the organization shouted. Hanin and two other children had reached a waiting minivan. She was about to step into it when she froze, confused about whose orders to follow. One wrong move and she feared she might be shot—again.

The rebels were angry and clearly hadn't expected this early-morning rescue operation. They pointed their guns at the prisoners streaming out of the church, forcing them back indoors. Hanin, too, was led back inside, and the men from the organization were angrily told to leave.

Hanin burst into tears. So, too, did many of the women and children. They had come so close to being rescued. If only the guards hadn't woken up, the prisoners might be free of this place. If only they had moved faster, or quieter, or, or, or . . . but none of it changed their reality. Hanin and the other fifty-three prisoners were still being held in the church.

Later that night, the prisoners were ordered into waiting minivans, this time by their rebel captors. They drove a short distance before being led into a small, stuffy underground basement. Another move, another prison, but they didn't stay in this one long. The guards were replaced with other men whom Hanin and her fellow captives had never seen before. The trio they had come to know must have been punished for falling asleep on the job, Hanin figured, but she didn't care what happened to them. That was not her concern.

The basement wasn't really big enough for fifty-four women and children, but they were squeezed into the space nonetheless. Somehow, Hanin managed to fall asleep, only to once again be jolted awake by the sounds of people moving around her and orders being yelled. Some of the prisoners were being told to leave the basement. The space started to empty until only fifteen people, including Hanin and her cousin Sally, remained inside. Where had the others been taken? Were they released or had they met an uglier fate? The rebels hadn't mentioned a prisoner swap. So many questions without answers, only fears that grew stronger with every passing minute.

After some time, how much time it was difficult to tell, Hanin heard the sound of a key turning in a lock. An armed man was in the basement, telling the captives to get out. Another minivan. It was dark outside. When the wheels stopped, the small group was led upstairs to a new location. The first batch of prisoners, who had been moved earlier, was already inside.

The next morning, Hanin and the other captives were surprised to see the familiar faces of the same people from the organization standing outside their new prison.

This time, the unarmed men from the organization didn't seem to be in a rush and the new armed guards outside were working with them, not against them. "They told us we were going to be released," Hanin said. "'Get ready. The minivans are ready for you. They're waiting outside.' I didn't believe it. Was it true?" Or was it yet another empty promise, a desperate hope that would soon be dashed like all the others? There was only one way to find out.

Hanin and the other captives rushed outside and into the waiting minivans. Nobody stopped them, and nobody fired into the air. "We were so happy!" she said. They drove to a village near the Turkish border called Ain al-Bayda, where they were told to wait in a house. It was a regular house belonging to a family with children, not another makeshift prison. Hanin and the other prisoners were no longer in the custody of the armed rebels but with the mysterious people of the unknown organization. They didn't know what sort of deal had been worked out among the anti-Assad factions and didn't much care for the details. The main thing was that this time the promise of freedom seemed real.

The family whose home Hanin and the others were

staying in made a huge lunch for the fifty-four captives. For the first time in years, Hanin and the others were treated like guests, not prisoners. That evening, they were driven along winding mountain roads, from Ain al-Bayda down to the informal border between rebel-held Syria and the parts of the country still controlled by the government.

It was early morning, the sun shaking off the shadows of its slumber, when the minivans reached their destination. It was February 8, 2017. Hanin could see waiting for them in the no-man's-land between the two warring sides a row of Red Crescent vehicles. (The Red Crescent is the same independent humanitarian organization as the Red Cross. The only difference is the name; in Muslim countries, the group uses the Islamic symbol of the crescent instead of the Christian cross.) Hanin could barely contain her excitement. After so many false promises, this one was real! The prisoners were transferred into the custody of the Red Crescent and driven to a hotel in government-controlled territory somewhere in Latakia.

Hanin had been freed in a prisoner exchange. The fifty-four Alawite captives were swapped for fifty-five

Sunni women being held by the regime. Hanin called her father, Talal, on his landline in Damascus. For the first time in years, she spoke to him not as a prisoner begging to be released but as a girl talking to her baba.

Talal drove straight up from Damascus to Latakia but wasn't allowed to see Hanin. The former prisoners were not yet to be released into the custody of their families. There was somebody else they had to see. The next day, Hanin and the other women and children met President Assad and his wife, Asma. The people from the organization had brought them all new clothes. Hanin was pleased to be rid of the drab outfit she'd been forced to wear in captivity. She tore off the headscarf and, for the first time in years, allowed her brown hair to flow to her waist. She listened, dressed in gray pants and a sky-blue sweatshirt, as Assad welcomed them home, kissed and greeted every person. "There wasn't a day that passed when people weren't looking for you," he told them. Assad said he knew what the women and children had suffered in captivity: "You lived in a warped society, without any humanity whatsoever. For three years you lived with people who know nothing of decency, of education, of civilization."

Soon after, Hanin and the other women and children were reunited with their families. Talal, Jawa, and her baby brother waited to greet Hanin. "When I saw him, Baba was crying and I was crying. I couldn't stop the tears," Hanin said. They drove home to Mezzeh 86, to an apartment bursting with friends and neighbors who welcomed Hanin home. Days later, Talal posted photos on Facebook of Hanin playing with her siblings in a park, and penned these words:

> *Good morning*
> *You have returned Hanin and language betrays me*
> *The letters celebrate a wild ibex accosting its hunter*
> *I cannot write anything except I am born again seeing you*
> *Good morning to friends and enemies, you are my brothers*
> *Good morning, Hanin*
> > *There was no morning before you or after you.*

EPILOGUE

By 2019, the outcome of the Syrian war was clear, even though the conflict had not yet ended. Assad had won. The Syrian president, with the help of his Russian, Iranian, and Lebanese Hizballah allies, had taken back control of most of Syria. Nobody really knew exactly how many Syrians had been killed in years of war. Millions were displaced, either internally, living in dismal makeshift camps scattered throughout the country, or beyond Syria's borders. The war had unraveled the state. It had divided Syria into a patchwork of pro- and anti-Assad areas and, in the process, reduced entire villages, towns, and cities to rubble.

The extremist ISIS group, which in earlier years had set up what it called a caliphate (or an Islamic state) in eastern Syria (as well as parts of Iraq), was militarily defeated. An assortment of groups—including a Western-led coalition and its fighter pilots, Iraqi security forces, Syrian rebel fighters, and Assad soldiers—had driven ISIS out of its territory. Everybody, it seemed, even those on opposite sides of the Syrian war, had battled the extremists. Kurdish-led Syrian forces took control of the parts of eastern Syria that ISIS had previously ruled, and although they were against Assad, some elements were open to speaking with him and possibly returning to the government's fold. In October 2019, Kurdish forces were driven out by Turkish-backed fighters. Assad, for his part, vowed to retake every inch of Syria.

Assad's hard-core rebel opponents, the ones who refused to reconcile with a regime that had spent years trying to kill them, were largely restricted to Idlib Province, where Ruha and her family lived. There had been a mini war between Assad's opponents that pitted Islamic extremists like ISIS and Jabhat al-Nusra against more moderate rebels like the Free Syrian Army. Although they were all technically against Assad, they were also against one another—ISIS and Jabhat al-Nusra even fought each other. It was a complicated, messy battlefield with many different players. The extremists of Jabhat al-Nusra had come out on top in the battle for control of rebel-held areas. The group changed its name several times and claimed to have split from Al-Qaeda, but it hadn't changed its goals, regardless of what it called itself. It still wanted to turn Syria into a conservative Islamic state. It was the main power broker in Idlib Province, trapping many families like Ruha's between two sides they despised—Assad's and the Islamic extremists.

After their return to Syria in 2016, Ruha, Alaa, and their family lived in the farmhouse along with Aunt Mariam. The family complex was still in disrepair, a fact that hurt Ruha's heart. Despite its poor state, one of Ruha's aunts nonetheless moved into the family complex, because her home had been bombed and she and her family had nowhere else to go. The farmhouse wasn't an option—it was barely big enough for Ruha's immediate family. On Valentine's Day, 2019, Grandmother Zahida, who was in her nineties, passed away peacefully in her bed. Maysaara continued to work on the farm, employing relatives and other locals, although the factory that he had proudly built was destroyed in a regime air strike. He and his workers were lucky to survive. They had all been in the building just minutes before it was blown up.

"Everything is gone," Maysaara said of the piles of

twisted metal and rubble that were once his pride and joy. "God alone protected us. How else did we not die?"

Ruha and Alaa readjusted to life in wartime, which meant living with the constant fear of regime air strikes.

The simple act of going to school was dangerous. Both sisters were in secondary school now, and their all-girls' facility was in the heart of Saraqeb, close to the souq. The souq was a frequent target of regime air strikes and people were often killed in the market as they shopped for groceries and other essentials. Sometimes the rockets would land near Ruha and Alaa's school.

"We would go to school, but when the shelling started up again, we had to stop going," Alaa said. The girls studied at home from their textbooks and tried to limit their time in school, although they still attended classes when they could. The one thing they could not do from home was take exams.

"Baba was very scared and he'd say, 'Don't go [to school for exams], I don't want to lose you. It's too dangerous,'" Ruha said. "We were also scared for Baba, because he would drive us to and from school. Alaa and I were scared that something would happen to him on the road." Ruha said that, once, after Maysaara dropped his daughters off at school to take their final exams of 2019, "about half an hour later, we heard that there had been shelling on the road, and we later learned that the car in front of Baba was struck, but somehow the rocket didn't explode. It could have been Baba's car, or the rocket could have burst into flames. We are very worried that something would happen to Baba because of us, because we made him drive us to school."

There were other dangers, too, at school, mainly from the Islamic extremists who were prevalent in Idlib Province. They had returned to Saraqeb, and one of their many bases was not far from the girls' school. The extremists enforced a dress code and would periodically swoop into the school to see if the students were complying. The girls had to wear long, belted overcoats that extended down to their ankles, or a flowing black abaya. A face veil was also preferred although not obligatory. A coat above the knee was considered "short" and would result in threats of punishments, including an interrogation.

"Baba didn't make us dress conservatively, but we started dressing the same as the community we are living in, and it's become more conservative," Ruha said. "We still wear pants, but to avoid gossip we dress like them in a long overcoat. We don't cover our faces. We both told Baba that we'd stop going to school altogether if [the extremists] forced us to cover our faces."

Alaa said that "at first I would go in what they consider a short coat, on purpose, just above my knee, because I didn't want to wear what they wanted me to wear, but then Baba didn't want me to get into trouble so he bought me a long coat."

"It's like that's their job now," Ruha said of the extremists. "Instead of fighting, they want to focus on the length of our coats."

The best thing about school was that it enabled the sisters to reconnect with some of their old friends, although many more were gone: They'd either left Syria and become refugees or were displaced elsewhere in the country, or had been killed. Ruha was reunited with her old friend Serene, the one she used to walk to school with, but time and distance had diluted their friendship. Although Ruha and Serene were once again in the same class, both girls had changed, shaped by their different experiences. Ruha and her family had spent several years in Turkey. Serene had stayed in Syria throughout the war and was now an orphan. She had lost most of her family.

Serene "is very attached to the friends that stayed in Syria with her, not the ones like me who left," Ruha said. "After her family died, she became very close to the friends who were still around her. I don't think she accepts the idea of letting anybody else into her life, even somebody like me who she knew before. We talk, our desks are close to each other, but we're not *friends* friends. We took different paths in life."

In Damascus, by 2019, the concrete security checkpoints that once choked the city's streets, blocking off key roads and creating traffic jams, had been removed. Victory looked like roads open to traffic in a more confident Syrian capital, one where the threat of car bombs and other attacks had diminished as the regime stamped its authority on the former rebel-held territories circling Damascus. But victory also looked like long walls plastered with the photos of thousands of dead soldiers and security men, a visual reminder of the sacrifices on the regime side.

After years of a vicious war, Assad's Syria and its Baathist system were still intact, as were the many intelligence and security agencies. The prisons were full to bursting with Assad's opponents. So, too, were the graveyards. Although rubble was being cleared from some war-ravaged neighborhoods and cities, many more were still wastelands. Millions of Syrians were unable to return home because they no longer had homes to return to, or because they feared being arrested and disappeared by the regime. The economy was crippled by war and international sanctions against the Assad regime. The Syrian pound was weak and unstable. Inflation was rampant, driving up the cost of goods and services, which only made the gas and fuel shortages worse. Talal often waited hours in line to refill his car's gas tank. Sometimes, he said, the lines were so long that drivers would park their cars at the gas station overnight, in the order they arrived, to resume their place in the queue the next morning.

Life was harder, but for Hanin and Jawa, the hardships were minor inconveniences compared to what they'd survived. They were alive and reunited with their father after years of captivity. They were home again, and that was all that mattered. The summer after Hanin was released, in 2017, she and her sister Jawa went to summer camp. They enjoyed the break and felt like regular girls again, playing with other young people their age, having fun and enjoying the summer.

The girls enrolled in school in Damascus, not in their old primary school (they were too old for that despite the fact that they'd missed years of schooling) but a new high school. With a lot of work and the help of sympathetic teachers and tutors who condensed lessons, they soon caught up to years of missed lessons. Hanin returned to playing the piano. She said the instrument soothed her. As a tribute to her dead sister, Lojayn, Hanin also began studying the violin. Jawa finally chose an instrument— the piano—and began lessons.

Their home in the village of Blouta, the place that was supposed to be a haven but instead became their hell, remains a painful memory for the sisters. They have visited it several times. The property is in ruins. "It looked so different," Jawa said the first time she went back after her kidnapping, while Hanin was still kept prisoner. "I just wanted to see my house again, the place I used to sleep and eat and play and read, but when I saw it, I cried. I was too scared to go in alone. I went in with my cousins. I wanted to go in case I found something, a memento."

She found her sister Lojayn's broken violin. Its strings were missing, its neck snapped. The instrument lay on its case, surrounded by shards of broken glass, a strewn pack of playing cards, and other household items. Jawa gave the broken violin to her father. She saw other things, too, that were painful reminders of what had happened that night, like the red Adidas jacket, she said, "that I had been wearing that same day before they took us." She found her shell collection and took it home with her to Mezzeh 86.

Hanin, too, returned to the house in Blouta after she was released. She saw her electronic keyboard tossed outside, its synthesizer smashed as if it had been stepped on, several of its black and white keys missing. "I don't like the village and I'm not happy there," Hanin said. "I don't like going there at all. It's where my mother and sister died. Many of my family members were killed in the village." Blouta, she said, "just isn't the same anymore. It will never be the same to me."

Sometimes, Hanin says, she sinks into dark thoughts about what happened to her and her family. "I always think about why my mother and sister and my uncles and other relatives died." She doesn't have a good answer.

She doesn't understand why and how a Syrian could kill another Syrian, including women and children, because they were perceived to be "on the other side." She still wonders about what could make a person hate another person to that degree, and how she and her family were caught in their country's savage war. "I didn't know that there were armed men who would come and kill civilians, farmers, that they would enter villages and homes and kill people," she said.

There were armed men on the regime side, too, who did the same thing but on a bigger scale, using the war machinery of a state. They killed civilians, farmers, and others. They also entered villages and homes and killed people perceived to be "on the other side" or they obliterated them from the skies in air strikes. Ruha's family and her hometown of Saraqeb experienced that, as did every area with an anti-Assad rebel presence.

In the summer of 2019, after a protracted lull, the regime air strikes in Idlib picked up again. Assad's forces were pushing into the province, although it wasn't yet an all-out offensive. Maysaara sent his wife, Manal, and their children to Turkey, while he stayed behind in Syria. He and Manal wondered what to do. Should the family try to settle in Turkey or should they all return to Syria? What if they were trapped in Syria and the fighting got worse? What if they went to Turkey and could not return home? And what about their extended family?

Ruha and her siblings were once again refugees, once again living in limbo, once again separated from their extended family and their father by borders and conflict. In summer 2019, they spent the Muslim Eid al-Adha holiday apart. Baba was stuck in Syria, and Ruha and her mother and siblings were in Turkey. Ruha hoped Baba would soon join them in the safety of Turkey. She was relieved to be away from the Syrian war zone. She remembered the many times her family struggled to try to find safety where there was none.

Once, she said, during a particularly intense round of air strikes, her family huddled under an olive tree near their farmhouse because, she said, "we figured that was the safest place. If a rocket or bomb fell there, it would land in soft dirt, not hard concrete. If anything, we'd be covered in dirt, not trapped under the concrete ruins of our farmhouse. Staying in the house is usually more dangerous. These years that we were in Syria were spent in fear. Constant fear," Ruha said. "It's like we were just sitting there waiting for death, wondering where it would come from—the skies, or a rocket or a tank shell or something else. That's it." In Turkey, Ruha said, "we can relax, we don't have to worry about such things. We can focus on studying, not wondering if Baba is going to die on the way home after he drops us off at school. We want to get a good education. We want to focus on our studies, to not lose the opportunity for a better future, to make something of ourselves. Nothing is for free. Everything comes at a cost and the cost of continuing our education in peace is that we can't do that in our country, near our families and in Saraqeb."

Her sister Alaa was less enthusiastic about being back in Turkey. Although she said she was also "very tired" of the worries of living in a war zone, she was deeply attached to Saraqeb and her extended family there, and didn't want to face the stigma of being a stranger in a foreign land. "I don't really want to be in Turkey," she said. "I don't want to be called a refugee."

For Ruha, exile was a bitter but realistic fact that she had accepted. "We know that the regime isn't going anywhere anymore and that there's nothing we can do about it," she said. "Syria is gone. The regime will take back everything, if not now, later. They will retake everything. I often get into arguments with Baba over this. I tell him, 'Enough, Baba. Sell everything in Saraqeb. At the end of the day, we will all have to flee, the regime will retake everything.' He refuses to sell, and he gets angry at me."

"And so do I!" Alaa said. "It's our hometown. We can't cut all ties to it. It's where our roots are."

"The regime will retake all of Idlib," Ruha replied. "Should we wait for them at home, for them to come and take Baba or worse?"

The two groups of sisters—Hanin and Jawa, and Ruha and Alaa—had survived horrors that many adults cannot even imagine. After all their trials and tribulations, Jawa said she is simply happy to once again have "a normal life" with her family. She doesn't dwell on the past. Hanin, too, prefers to look to the future. "I've put everything behind my back, and I'm thinking about my future, I'm working toward having a better future," Hanin said. She isn't yet sure what she wants to be when she grows up, "perhaps a doctor or an engineer," but she is determined that whatever she chooses, "I want to be and study something exceptional."

Hanin—who as a prisoner in 2016 once said, "I think about my future, which has been completely destroyed. I wanted to be a doctor, but it's impossible now that I'll be a doctor"—is not only back in school but in 2019 attained the highest marks in her grade to finish first among her peers. Her experiences, she says, have taught her one key thing about life and about herself: "For certain," Hanin said, "there is nothing that is impossible anymore."

For Ruha, the issue of "what she wants to be when she grows up" is too far in the future to contemplate. Her more immediate concern is to reunite her family and that Baba Maysaara will join them in Turkey. Alaa hopes for the same, as well as a sense of stability. "We don't know if we are going to stay here and live in Turkey, or if we will go back to Saraqeb," Alaa said. "It depends on the situation. Once we know what country we will be in, then we can start thinking about hopes and dreams and what we want to do with our lives."

After years of war and exile, Ruha said the biggest lesson she has learned is "to live one day at a time because nobody knows what tomorrow might bring . . .

"Perhaps nobody can understand what we've experienced unless they lived it," Ruha said, reflecting on all the years that have passed since those first protests in Syria in 2011. "Maybe people will read our story and not believe it, but it happened to us. What I know for sure is that we have to live. We want to live. We can't let the past, and thinking about what we lost, hold us back. Our lives can't stop at a particular point. We must go on and we will."

AUTHOR'S NOTE

This is a book of firsthand reporting, investigated over six years and countless trips inside Syria. I am a journalist who has reported for many years from across the Middle East and South Asia. In early 2011, I covered the revolutions in Tunisia and Egypt and then made my way in late February to Syria, where I witnessed one of the earliest protests in the capital. It was a small gathering of some two hundred people outside the Libyan embassy in Damascus, held in solidarity with Libyan protesters who at the time were trying to bring down their own regime. The protest was violently dispersed by Assad's forces.

Since that day, I have focused almost exclusively on the Syria story. In the summer of 2011, I learned that I was blacklisted by the Syrian regime, but not as a journalist. Instead, I was branded a spy for several foreign states, placed on the wanted lists of three of the four main intelligence agencies in Damascus, and banned from entering the country. This forced me to focus on the rebel side by illegally trekking across the Turkish border into northern Syria, although I still managed a few trips to government-held areas.

I knew and could describe many of the smuggling routes into Syria from Turkey because I had taken them. I am one of those journalists who wanted to see for herself what was happening in Syria, without government minders, and I did not want to rely on social media posts to try to understand what was happening on the rebel side. There is no substitute for reporting from a place and witnessing events yourself.

I attended demonstrations in various towns and cities, spent time with Free Syrian Army fighters on numerous front lines across the country, interviewed Jabhat al-Nusra commanders, civil activists, families caught in the middle of it all, and many refugees scattered across Turkey, Lebanon, Jordan, and in Europe.

After the start of the revolution, I entered Syria clandestinely so many times that I lost count. For years, I was either inside Syria or on its periphery, interviewing Syrians before reentering their country, spending no more than a week to ten days a month at my home base in neighboring Lebanon. The accounts in this book are in part based on reporting presented in my longer Syria book, *No Turning Back: Life, Loss, and Hope in Wartime Syria,* published in March 2018 by W. W. Norton.

Ruha and her extended family generously opened their homes and their hearts to me, allowing me to witness their highs and lows over six tumultuous years. I wasn't with them during those first raids when Ruha opened the door to security forces, accounts re-created by interviewing every member of her family who was in the house on those two days, but I was present or in direct contact with them for just about every other event thereafter. I was with Maysaara as he returned home to Saraqeb in July 2012 after recuperating from gunshot wounds. I watched Ruha and her siblings change into their new Turkish clothes and how excited they were that Baba was finally home. I spent a lot of time with Ruha in their family complex and spent many a night in their tiled courtyard and in their basement during shelling.

I was in the Saraqeb hospital in summer 2012 as the dead and wounded arrived on that terrible day when rebels battled for the Kaban Checkpoint, and I stood near that little girl as she was being operated on without anesthetic.

I was with Ruha and her family as they sneaked across the Syrian border into Turkey on that harrowing journey, and I shared their first night in Turkey with them in a small, cramped room. I was with Aunt Mariam and Uncle Mohammad as they cowered in the basement with other relatives, listening to the sounds of shells exploding all around them, and I was with the women sitting in Grandmother Zahida's living room on that cold winter's night with no electricity, listening to them debate what kind of Syria they wanted and their fears about Islamists.

The account of the unexploded canister and the chemical attack on Saraqeb was based on interviews with local activists (including unpublished footage privately shared with me, showing one activist hiding the canister) as well as a December 13, 2013, report by the Organisation for the Prohibition of Chemical Weapons (OPCW) titled *United Nations Mission to Investigate Allegations of the Use of Chemical Weapons in the Syrian Arab Republic.*

Maysaara called me when he stood outside the smuggler's office in the Turkish coastal city of Mersin, sharing his thoughts about whether he should risk getting to Europe or stay in Turkey. I spent a lot of time with his family in Turkey and returned to Syria in 2016 to see

Maysaara's factory and the life he was building for his wife and children while he waited for them to join him.

I met Talal in Beirut weeks after his family was kidnapped from their home in Blouta in August 2013. I had previously been with rebel fighters along the Latakia front line soon after the families were captured and the eleven Alawite villages were seized. I remained in contact with Talal and with others whose families were in rebel captivity for years, as well as the activists trying to free them. Their plight was also detailed in an October 10, 2013, Human Rights Watch report titled *You Can Still See Their Blood*. I knew the Jabhat al-Nusra emirs in charge of the prisoners' fate and the Free Syrian Army unit keeping watch over them.

I spent time in Dr. Rami's field clinic in Salma over the years and traveled with him and his team as they treated people from their three remaining ambulances after the field clinic was destroyed. I saw Talal's young niece, Reema, when she was carried into the Salma clinic by a foreign fighter. I was in that ambulance in 2016 as it climbed through Idlib's hills, headed to the church where Hanin and the other women and children were imprisoned. I saw Hanin in captivity, the only journalist to do so, and I taped her short message to her father. In 2016, I managed to get permission to briefly enter Damascus, despite the multiple arrest warrants against me, to attend a government-sponsored conference. I slipped away from the conference to go to Mezzeh 86 and let Talal hear his daughter's taped voice. I interviewed Jawa and later Hanin and her cousin Sally about their experiences. President Assad's comments in 2017 after their release were filmed and uploaded to the internet. I knew some of the many changing interlocutors on both sides of an issue I had followed closely since the raid in August 2013. Like everything in this book, my access came from being there and sticking with the story.

ABOUT THE AUTHOR

Rania Abouzeid has reported from the Middle East and South Asia for many years. A fluent Arabic speaker, she has written for *TIME*, *The New Yorker*, *National Geographic*, *Politico*, and a host of other publications. Her print and television journalism has been honored with numerous awards, including the 2015 Michael Kelly Award, the 2014 George Polk Award for Foreign Reporting, and the 2013 Kurt Schork Award in International Journalism. Rania's first book for adults, *No Turning Back: Life, Loss, and Hope in Wartime Syria,* also garnered awards recognition. She lives in Beirut and can be found online at raniaabouzeid.com.